certain uncertainty

DES DEARLOVE

Co-founder, Thinkers 50

certain uncertainty

LEADING WITH
AGILITY AND **RESILIENCE**
IN AN UNPREDICTABLE WORLD

WILEY

For general information on our other products and services or for technical support, please contact our Customer Care Department within the United States at (800) 762-2974, outside the United States at (317) 572-3993 or fax (317) 572-4002.

Wiley also publishes its books in a variety of electronic formats. Some content that appears in print may not be available in electronic formats. For more information about Wiley products, visit our web site at www.wiley.com.

Library of Congress Cataloging-in-Publication Data is Available:

ISBN 9781394153459 (Cloth)
ISBN 9781394153466 (ePub)
ISBN 9781394153473 (ePDF)

Cover image(s): Paul McCarthy
Cover design: © GETTY IMAGES | OSAKAWAYNE STUDIOS

Printed and bound by CPI Group (UK) Ltd, Croydon, CR0 4YY

C004926_140323

*This book is dedicated to the memory of Alessandro Di Fiore,
whose insights and friendship continue to inspire.*

About Thinkers50

Thinkers50 is the world's most reliable resource for identifying, ranking, and sharing the leading management and business ideas of our age. Since 2001, we've been providing access to ideas with the power to make a positive difference in the world.

The Thinkers50 definitive ranking of management thinkers is published every two years. Its Distinguished Achievement Awards, which recognize the very best in management thinking and practice, have been described by the *Financial Times* as the "Oscars of management thinking."

Contents

Foreword

The only certainty today is uncertainty.

I imagine you've read sentences like this too many times to count over the past few years. But when was the last time you stopped to consider the profound implications of this simple observation? For students of management, like me, one implication is that much of what we have long taken for granted about what good managers do to ensure excellence no longer holds true. Management is badly in need of new thinking (and new action). For that, we need a diverse set of ideas and experiments. And for stewarding both with insight and curiosity, we can thank Thinkers50's remarkable founders, Des Dearlove and Stuart Crainer. It is a privilege to be asked to write a foreword for Des's new book—with its engaging, thoughtful, provocative chapters by up-and-coming leaders in the study and practice of management.

Despite their diverse content, these works all share common threads. Notably, you will read more than once that the increasingly uncertain and interconnected world of work calls for us to adopt an agile and flexible mindset. Diversity and connection and conversation also emerge as critical themes. Consider that a primary requirement for today's managers is staying informed, which means constant updating and adapting. Yet the inherently collaborative nature of this activity may be underappreciated. The only way to stay informed is to convene and listen to diverse voices. And the only way to make sense of new information is to approach it with curiosity and rigor—to find the signals amidst the noise. You could say that success in an uncertain world depends upon an ability to make high quality bets. And, high quality bets, in turn, depend upon high-quality conversations. Progress in uncertain times is a team sport!

Research on teaming, to which I have contributed, underlines the importance of being open to new ideas and perspectives. Historically, management training emphasized control, conformity, and efficiency. Today, the emphasis has shifted to empowerment, diversity, and innovation. It's not that efficiency and reliable processes are completely absent in the new management landscape but rather that their effect on organizational performance is far less. Today's primary leadership task is thus helping people make the shifts in mindset and behavior that support the agility, experimentation, and teamwork that increasingly drive performance. And this brings us to the need for psychological safety.

Perhaps you've long considered meetings to be a waste of time and groups as places where good ideas go to die, but our dependence on others for information, ideas, and concerns is increasingly evident. The success of any organization thus depends on people's willingness to speak up and speaking up occurs in an environment of psychological safety. Without it, the behaviors that underlie collaboration and innovation—but also risk management—are rarely practiced with any kind of consistency. These behaviors have become all the more important as the world becomes more complex and multicultural. This again is what makes this volume so important.

It's natural to be anxious about the challenges that lie ahead. But no leader has all the answers. So long as leaders actively invite others in to help solve the problems their organizations face, a path forward will be found. Navigating uncertainty requires input from diverse sources. Making this happen starts with leaders who are open-minded and transparent, prepared to acknowledge that they don't have all the answers, and willing to listen to and work with others. Even when we fully recognize the intellectual merits of these statements, it can be emotionally challenging to put them into practice. Yet, we still need to act—moving ahead with purpose rather than being paralyzed by indecision. The key is to remain open to changing circumstances and willing to pivot at short notice, motivated by new ideas and possibilities.

In that spirit, this book offers fresh thinking and distilled wisdom from the brightest new management minds. This is a book of ideas with power for practice; its many authors appreciate both the intellectual and the emotional challenges of being a leader. Although they point to skills and practices that can be difficult to develop, there is much in the pages ahead to help you do just that. The world continues to become more complex and uncertain. And this is why this book is essential reading for leaders everywhere.

Amy C. Edmondson
Cambridge, MA
January 2023

Introduction

Certain Uncertainty

It was the best of times. It was the worst of times. It was the age of wisdom. It was the age of foolishness. It was the epoch of belief. It was the epoch of incredulity. It was the season of light. It was the season of darkness. It was the spring of hope. It was the winter of despair.

The opening lines of *A Tale of Two Cities*[1] seem hauntingly prescient. Charles Dickens could have been writing about our present day. As we emerge from the fog of the Covid-19 pandemic into a world threatened by a previously unthinkable war in Europe and a global climate crisis, and reflect on what we have learned, only one thing seems certain—that we live in an age of uncertainty.

Every year, the *Collins English Dictionary* publishes its 10 words or phrases of the year.[2] The list acts as a barometer of what's going on in the world. It "reflects our ever-evolving language and the preoccupations of those who use it." Lockdown and fake news have all featured in previous years, and 2022's list includes the terms "quiet quitting"— the practice of doing no more work than one is contractually obliged to do. But the winner—the word of the year in 2022? "Permacrisis: An extended period of instability and insecurity, especially one resulting from a series of catastrophic events."

It is this unsettled and unsettling new reality that we must all confront. And yet, it is not all doom and gloom. As Dickens reminds us, with uncertainty comes opportunity: a spring of hope. With ambiguity comes new choices and fresh ways of interpreting our place in the world. Yet, to nurture the green shoots of hope and replenish ourselves and our world we will need to reimagine it. That will take a new sort of leadership.

An Unpredictable World

For much of the last century we have assumed that markets, indeed entire nations, operate in a state of relative stability. From time to time, they are subjected to destabilizing forces—natural disasters, economic depression, war—or, as we have seen lately, disease. But once the threat had passed, the traditional role of leaders was to return society to something approaching the previous steady state.

This was a world where companies could make plans in the belief that they would still be relevant in, say, five years' time, and that business would continue relatively unchanged. Today, however, we live in what has been described as a VUCA world, an environment characterised by *v*olatility, *u*ncertainty, *c*omplexity, and *a*mbiguity.

In the last few years, we have seen a stream of disruptions to business as usual, most notably Covid-19 and the war in Ukraine. Add in the threat of global warming, oil price volatility, a cost-of-living crisis, rising inflation, plus the ever-present threat of another pandemic, and it is clear that the shocks keep on coming.

In his book, *Fooled by Randomness*,[3] Nassim Taleb described shocks to the financial system as "black swans"—unforeseen events that had a disproportionate impact. In his follow-up book *The Black Swan*,[4] Taleb extended the metaphor to other "undirected and unpredicted" events, including the advent of the Internet, the personal computer, and the end of the Soviet Union. What all have in common, he proposed, is three attributes: rarity, extreme impact, and retrospective (but not prospective) predictability.

First, a black swan event is an outlier—outside the realm of normal expectations. Second, it carries extreme impact. Third, we create explanations for why it happened *after the event* making it explainable and predictable. According to Taleb's definition, then, disruptive new technologies and other as yet unknown events, are also part and parcel of the external environment in which leaders must operate.

Business as usual is a phrase we have become used to, but in the post-Covid world, it seems like a distant memory. Some might yearn for the old ways and the old certainties—but business was never certain; predictability was always an illusion. Recent events have simply shattered that illusion.

What have the pandemic and other global shocks taught us about leadership? If nothing else, they have shown up the futility of pretending we can control the world around us. The old model of the omniscient leader who knows all the answers has been thoroughly debunked and shown up for the myth it always was.

What we need now are leaders who are humbler; who are willing to admit they don't know what's around the next corner but are ready to respond to whatever it might prove to be. Leaders who we can believe in because they are honest about their shortcomings, and open to challenge. Leaders who are inclusive and recognize that diversity in all its forms is a strength and a necessity. In short, what we need is a new sort of leader who can help us navigate through turbulent and unpredictable times.

To be able to respond better to unforeseen events, we need to build resilience and agility into our lives, including the way business operates. Change is now a constant, disruption is to be expected, and requires an adaptable response.

We can't go back. We must go forwards. So, what do the next generation of leaders need to know about living with Certain Uncertainty? That's the question we put to the select group of business thinkers who make up the Thinkers50 Radar with Community. This book is their response—a curated collection of short essays addressed to the leaders of the present and future, to help them not only to survive but also to thrive in these uncertain times. We hope that the advice and fresh thinking they contain will help you—the leaders of tomorrow—on your journey.

I leave you with the words of one of the all-time-great management thinkers, C.K. Prahalad, who topped the Thinkers50 Ranking in 2009 and 2011. "Leadership is not an extrapolation of the current situation into the future but imagining the future . . . You cannot lead unless you are future oriented. Leadership is about change—and leadership is about hope."[5]

About Thinkers50

Thinkers50 is the world's most reliable resource for identifying, ranking, and sharing the leading management ideas of our age. It began life in 2001 as a ranking of the world's most influential management thinkers. Today, it publishes four authoritative lists:

- *Thinkers50 Ranking*: the original and pre-eminent global ranking of management and business thinkers since 2001.
- *Thinkers50 Distinguished Achievement Awards*: the "Oscars of management thinking" (*Financial Times*),[6] presented every two years for outstanding contributions in multiple award categories.
- *Thinkers50 Radar Class*: the 30 management and business thinkers to watch, published annually, every January.
- *Thinkers50 Management Hall of Fame*: the giants of management thinking whose ideas have made a lasting contribution to management and business. New inductees into the Hall of Fame are announced every September.

Notes

1. Charles Dickens, *A Tale of Two Cities* (Harmondsworth: Penguin Classics, 2003, originally published in 1859).
2. *Collins English Dictionary*, https://www.collinsdictionary.com/dictionary
3. Nassim Taleb, *Fooled by Randomness* (Harmondsworth: Penguin, 2007).
4. Nassim Taleb, *The Black Swan*, 2nd edition (Harmondsworth: Penguin, 2010).
5. C.K. Prahalad, author interview.
6. *Financial Times*, Not a Dry Eye in the Room, Andrew Hill, November 11, 2013.

Future Thinking

1

Resilient, Net Positive Leadership

Andrew Winston

It was the missing toilet paper that shook the world. The empty shelves that used to overflow with basic necessities finally woke us up to a harsh reality: our economy and our supply chains are fragile. The lack of resilience in the system created massive product losses and waste.

Supply chains are still a mess, in large part because they're not flexible. We built an economy that values efficiency above all, with limited redundancy or back-ups. That certainly keeps costs down and pleases shareholder value purists, but it's completely unfit for a volatile world. The pandemic was (we hope) a once-in-a-century phenomenon, but clearly the world is more uncertain than ever. Sudden shocks to the system are the norm. The only real way to prepare and lead is to build resilient organizations, communities, and economies.

At all scales, from companies to sectors to economies, leaders will need to change how they think about business. With a resilience lens—and I'll argue a sustainability lens as well—a company can greatly increase the odds of surviving, doing better than its peers in the face of deep change, and bouncing back faster from disruptions. From my work and observations of companies (and people) under stress, it seems that resilience is built on three fundamental pillars: (1) diversity and redundancy; (2) strong networks (i.e., friends you can trust); and (3) purpose or mission.

Before diving into those three areas, it's useful to look at the nature of today's volatility—that is, why are things so uncertain? It's a time when the only thing that's certain is uncertainty. We are in what the US military has called a "VUCA" world (*v*olatile, *u*ncertain, *c*omplex, and *a*mbiguous). Others might call it anarchy. It's also an era of exponential change, which is a challenge for we mortals who think in linear terms and at scales we can get our heads round (go ahead, create a mental picture of a trillion of anything).

Extraordinary forces are rocking the world, but three disruptions in particular—each tied to our greatest challenges—are driving unprecedented uncertainty: (1) biophysical collapse; (2) declining democracy and the breakdown of trust; and (3) rapid technological change.

"Biophysical" means the planet's species and resources which we utterly depend on; not just things we dig up, grow, or cut down, but also fundamental resources such as clean air and water and a relatively stable climate. Climate change and loss of biodiversity are the two greatest challenges we face. Extreme weather, which will accelerate until the world eliminates carbon emissions, is disrupting lives, communities, supply chains, and economies. And as species die off, we risk the collapse of the ecosystems and food pyramids that support our existence.

Second, democracy is in decline all over the world. There are clearly many causes, but the rise of inequality is a key driver. In the developed world, effectively all of the gains in income and wealth over the last 40 years has gone to the top 1% and even the top 0.1%. A 50-year experiment in neoliberal economics and obsession with shareholder value have created rapid growth and helped reduce the percentage in abject poverty. But it has left the middle behind. When people feel unheard or ignored, they become attracted to leaders who say, "I haven't forgotten you and I'll work for you—give me the power to fix it all." Unfortunately, those leaders are most often autocrats, demagogues, and narcissists who rarely care at all about the masses.

Finally, exponential technological capacity, and the "who really knows what will happen" potential of artificial intelligence (AI), create both radical opportunities and destabilizing risks. The algorithm-led misinformation campaigns feed the other disruptions, giving people reasons to doubt climate change or to fear change and hate the "other." Misinformation is breaking down trust, without which the world can hardly work on shared challenges. On the upside, technology can help solve our biggest problems. We are on the verge of massive improvements in the efficiency of buildings, transportation and logistics, manufacturing, food production, and waste reduction, and much more.

With this level of change and instability on multiple fronts, it's little wonder that piling on things like pandemics and the first war in Europe in 80 years can overload the system and leaders' ability to process and act. How can a leader help ensure near- or long-term success in the face of such unpredictability? Surely, building resilience is at the core. Resilience, most simply, means the ability to survive large swings in fortunes in any one part of a system (think portfolio theory in investments that has generally outperformed every other strategy), plus greater odds of bouncing back quicker than others, perhaps even stronger than before.

So back to the three fundamental pillars of resilience. Let's look at what they mean in today's world.

Diversity and Redundancy

It's a bad idea to have no back-up for things that are valuable—in essence, don't put all your eggs in one basket. Nassim Taleb, a leading thinker on risk, makes the case in his book, *Anti-Fragile*[1] that nature loves redundancies. Humans, he points out, have two of each of the body's critical systems (eyes, ears, lungs, kidneys, arms, and legs). That redundancy creates much more resilience.

Our economic systems are anything but resilient. The pandemic created a great irony when the world was short on medical equipment (or PPE). One of the largest producers of masks was in Wuhan, China, and major manufacturers of nasal swabs were based in Lombardy,

Italy—the two regions that were first overwhelmed by Covid and were shut down. From a purely economic perspective, with efficiency (and pleasing investors) at the core of all decisions, it makes sense to produce something in vast quantities in one place; the larger the scale, the lower the per unit cost. That keeps costs low . . . until that one place can't operate because everyone is sent home, or it's literally under water—in 2011, floods in Thailand shut down what was effectively the only source of key parts for hard drives and engines for major automakers. Extreme weather conditions like that are only increasing.

The pandemic exposed many flaws in our system. Even products that seemed to have diverse channels really didn't. Dairy farmers who produced milk for hotels, schools, and other institutions had to dump millions of gallons—they couldn't repurpose production and packaging to shift from bulk to gallon-scale offerings for supermarkets and homes.

Redundancy avoids those problems. But is there a catch? Is there a tension between the diversity that creates resilience and other goals, such as the overall reduction in material use and carbon emissions we desperately need to fight climate change, i.e., isn't it wasteful to have duplication? Maybe. It depends on what the redundancy protects against. In a famous example, after the *Exxon Valdez* oil spill in 1989, double hulls became the norm in the oil tanker world. More metal and expense, but it protects against vast environmental damage and wasted fuel.

Stepping further out, if we think about systems, diversity of all kinds offers strength and reduced total footprint. Having alternative pathways in a supply chain, for example, could make it less disruptive when one channel goes down. If you only have the one supply chain, rushing production elsewhere could produce material waste. Or consider some societal systems. In a city's metro area, having multiple ways to get around—cars, subway, bus, light rail—creates a lot of material production, but it can also greatly reduce emissions by giving people options besides their cars. Similarly, high speed rail can offset short plane journeys.

Finally, on the human side of the sustainability agenda, the case for diversity is more literal and clearer every day. A growing body of evidence[2] shows the vast business benefits of commitment to and action on diversity, equity, and inclusion (DEI). We've been talking about organizational level of resilience, but these principles apply on the personal leadership level too. As a leader or manager, it pays to bring in multiple voices with a range of perspectives by race, gender, abilities, and especially age. Listen to younger people who have a longer stake in where the world is heading.

Networks of Support

Modern economics and political systems have been based on some fairly egregious misreading of influential works. Adam Smith, for example, talked about the invisible hand much less than people realize, and when he did, it was in the service of equal distribution of resources, not hands off wealth accumulation. Similarly, Charles Darwin did not coin the phrase "survival of the fittest." His work pointed to the power of being adaptable (yes, resilient). In the intervening century and a half, the understanding of how nature works has shown something quite the opposite of the dog-eat-dog philosophy so many misread into Darwin.

Forests are not filled with individual trees competing for sunlight, but a much more nuanced dance and cooperation, facilitated by vast, incredibly complex networks of fungi connecting them all.[3] These networks, and countless symbiotic relationships in nature, create great strength and resilience. As in nature, organizational resilience comes from having a strong network around you. It's not just a buzzword to talk about serving stakeholders—they are the diverse, multi-faceted groups of people who support a company's existence. Building relationships with stakeholders provides support for volatile times. We all get by with a little help from our friends.

In life and in business, you build networks through genuine engagement, reciprocity, and trust (which is greatly enhanced by transparency). The strongest business for uncertain times will be one that stakeholders know is serving their needs. In a larger sense, it's a business that serves the world and improves the well-being of everyone it impacts. This kind of company, which profits from solving the world's problems, not creating them, is net positive, an idea laid out in the book *Net Positive*,[4] which I co-authored with former Unilever CEO Paul Polman.

In one of the most important moments in Unilever's 140-year history, networks saved the consumer products company. Kraft Heinz, owned by the private equity firm 3G Capital—widely known as an intense cost-cutter—attempted a hostile takeover of Unilever in 2017. Paul and his team knew that Unilever's focus on helping consumers live sustainable lives would not fit with 3G's culture. But holding that opinion would not be enough to fight off the takeover. No, it took a surprising range of stakeholders, including NGOs like Greenpeace and even labor unions, who spoke out to stop the merger; they wanted the company's genuine partnership with them on critical issues. Key investors also spoke out about their desire for long-term value creation, not just squeezing every penny out of every system in the short run.

In a nice parallel, when the pandemic hit, Unilever's new CEO Alan Jope reacted quickly to support the company's stakeholders. The company assured direct and indirect employees (like onsite cleaning or security) that they'd hold their jobs for months. It also set aside €500 million to help its business partners stay afloat, paying some suppliers early and extending credit to customers. Building trust with partners and critics alike is a long-term project, enhanced by demonstrating your values consistently every day.

Purpose and Mission

In *Net Positive*, after laying out the core principles, we argue that leaders can start the work of building a net positive company with two key related steps. First, we ask, "How much do you care?" And we mean you, the manager or leader. Part of what's been missing in business is humanity. The purely efficient shareholder value approach squeezes people out of the equation and values inhumanity—stock prices rise, and CEOs are celebrated whenever they announce major layoffs.

It enhances resilience for leaders and their organizations to work from a strong core of values and purpose. For the individual, purpose and duty come from a base level of caring about the world and those in it.

The former CEO and chairman of Mastercard, Ajay Banga, has talked about the need for leaders to demonstrate not just intelligence (IQ) or people skills (EQ), but "DQ," or decency quotient. Banga asks, do you care about those you manage and work with and for?[5]

Starting with humanity and having a larger mission than just yourself provides strength when the storms come. There are certainly counter-examples of greed and selfishness taking people far, but it doesn't mean that those people, or the systems they built, are resilient. When they topple, their former allies bail out quickly.

At the organizational level, resilience comes from a strong purpose as well—the core famously described in Collins and Porras' book, *Built to Last*.[6] Specifics like products and services, marketing, and even culture may shift around that core, but that reason for being should stick. Companies need to identify and cultivate that purpose. A strong purpose also attracts and retains talent, especially those in younger generations.

Years ago, I saw Xerox's then-CEO Anne Mulcahy talk about getting through near bankruptcy: "At the depths of our problems, we asked employees to roll up their sleeves, and most stayed because they believed in what the company stood for."[7]

Conclusion

In total, diversity, networks, and purpose create a powerful mix of strength and flexibility in uncertain times. In a world facing intertwined existential challenges, resilience comes from being part of the solutions, not the problems. It's also a great way to thrive as a business—tackling issues like climate change represents perhaps the greatest economic opportunity ever. Multi-trillion-dollar markets in buildings, transportation, food, and much more, are in play. A net positive business operates in those markets, even while serving existing customers' needs. A foot in the present, with deep investment in the future, is a powerful combination (auto companies, for example, are going all-in on the future of electric vehicles, while still delivering combustion engines for now).

A business that seeks the larger good—and pursues the true leadership of being net positive—is strong. The purpose is grounding, the stakeholder networks are ready to catch the company if it stumbles, and there's more diversity of thinking about products and services. The best way to prepare for a different and better future is to help create it. Solving the world's problems may be the only path to building a thriving company in an uncertain world. Improving the well-being of all and being on the right side of history feel pretty good, too.

Biography

Andrew Winston is one of the world's most widely read writers and thinkers on sustainable business. He is the co-author (with Paul Polman, the former CEO of Unilever) of *Net Positive: How Courageous Companies Thrive by Giving More Than They Take*. His books on sustainability strategy, including *Green to Gold* and *The Big Pivot*, have sold more than a quarter of a million copies in a dozen languages. In 2021, Thinkers50 ranked him among the 50 most influential business thinkers in the world.

Notes

1. Nassim Taleb, *Anti-Fragile* (Harmondsworth: Penguin, 2013).
2. https://www.nhbr.com/the-business-case-for-implementing-dei-diversity-equity-and-inclusion/.
3. Anne Casselman, "Strange but True: The Largest Organism on Earth Is a Fungus," *Scientific American*, October 4, 2007.
4. Paul Polman and Andrew Winston, *Net Positive: How Courageous Companies Thrive by Giving More Than They Take* (Boston: Harvard Business Review Press, 2021).
5. Stephanie Mehta, "Decency Quotient: How This CEO Frames Inclusive Capitalism for His Company," Fast Company, https://www.fastcompany.com/90424514/decency-quotient-how-this-ceo-frames-inclusive-capitalism-for-his-company.
6. Jim Collins and Jerry L. Porras, *Built to Last* (New York: Random House Business, 2005).
7. Daniel C. Esty and Andrew Winston, *Green to Gold* (Hoboken, NJ: Wiley, 2009), p. 91.

2

Leading Like a Futurist

Lisa Kay Solomon

Let's start with a mini thought experiment. Think back ten years, and fill in the following headlines:

- President _____ just announced _____.
- A new technology about _____ promises to _____.
- The most valuable company in the world is _____ because of its advantages in _____.

Maybe you have a great memory and easily filled in those blanks, or perhaps you did a quick internet search. Either way, it is possible to arrive at answers. The past is knowable.

Now, consider answering the same set of questions ten years from now. What methodologies and thinking processes would you use? How confident do you feel about your responses?

You may have felt a little uneasy thinking about how to answer those questions in a future context. How could you know the answers? How could anyone know? There are no facts about the future.

In a world of increasing volatility, uncertainty, complexity, and ambiguity—the "VUCA" world coined by U.S. military planners more than 30 years ago—the idea of predicting anything may feel like folly. And the days and decades ahead promise to deliver more VUCA than ever. It's likely that this present moment may be the least VUCA of days to come.

And yet, leaders must make decisions every day with incomplete, unknowable, and unreliable information. Leading in an increasingly VUCA world will require a new set of skills. We must think and act like futurists.

While none of us—not even the greatest AI—can predict the future with perfect accuracy, all of us can and must improve our ability to explore, evaluate, and communicate the future.

Futures thinking is not about predicting the future or getting the future "right." Futures thinking is a mindset, a set of methodologies, and a leadership stance that allow us to think expansively about what the future might look like in order to inform better decisions and actions in the present. Futures thinking enables us to have a long-term perspective while also allowing us to navigate ambiguity by holding seemingly competing, unfolding truths.

Humans are uniquely capable of envisioning and thinking about the future. Psychologists call this ability "prospection,"[1] and studies show that we practice it multiple times throughout our day. And yet, at the strategic and leadership levels, these practices have been overlooked, underdeveloped, and minimized as skills that can be taught and nurtured. We teach plenty of classes about history, but offer almost nothing on futures. How many business schools, for example, have required classes to help leaders imagine a broad range of possibilities through science fiction or mind wandering? Or offer workshops on exploring systems thinking, power dynamics, and constructs of time to better shape equitable futures? Or mandate classes on immersive, narrative storytelling to help leaders share futures in compelling and motivating ways?

For leaders who want to change the world and create lasting value for their shareholders and stakeholders, the skills required for leading like a futurist are essential capabilities. Honing our abilities to see, shape, and share the future not only can help us become more innovative, bold, and adaptive, it can also strengthen our personal resilience, flexibility, and responsiveness.

Seeing Bold Futures and the Big, Long Picture

In his 2013 *Harvard Business Review* article, "The Future Is at Odds with the Corporation," cultural anthropologist Grant McCraken said: "There is really only one way to live in a world of speed, surprise, noise, and responsiveness, and that's to visit the future frequently."[2]

For many leaders, "visiting the future" involves looking at business plans or financial projections for the next year. Looking at numbers provides a sense of security and safety, creating an illusion that the future can be predicted or even controlled. But it's all too easy to forget that those numbers are based on assumptions, past performance, and informed guesses, not hard evidence or guaranteed outcomes.

Then we are surprised when a macro event disrupts our estimates; or a global pandemic shuts down the world; or our workforce turns over in massive numbers; or a new technology "suddenly" matures and eats away at projected revenues and market share.

Seeing the future in more expansive ways requires being comfortable with investigating the unknown by discovering, questioning, and learning. It means exploring an unfolding trend through multiple sources and experiences, improving our ability to see interrelated systems and further-out implications, and embracing our curiosity, imagination, and ability to dream.

One way to better "see" futures is to incorporate a longer-term, outside-in view of how the world might change into strategic conversations and planning. This includes actively tracking macro forces, such as environmental, economic, technological, or demographic changes that will meaningfully shape our world. Futures thinkers go beyond reacting to the crisis of the moment and instead look for underlying patterns and dynamics. They are willing to suspend immediate questions of feasibility or financial viability with bold visions and applied imagination.

We can trace many of the great Silicon Valley "disruptors" to futurists who saw technology and social trends converging before others. Consider Jeff Bezos, who in 1997 called his company Amazon, after the largest river in the world. While most people doubted that selling discounted books online would ever live up to that name, Bezos held a much bolder vision of the "everything store" that would ultimately invent and dominate an entirely new market of cloud-based web services.

And Ann Wojcicki who, in 2005, began imagining a whole new market of personal genomics. This sprang from a dinner-party conversation where the guests compared notes on how different genetic make-ups can lead to tasting foods very differently. As a Wall Street financial analyst, she was intrigued by the long-term potential of the human genome project, a 13-year, $3 billion, scientific endeavor. Wojcicki realized that the technology would become cheaper and more powerful over time and a year later founded 23andMe. The company now has 12 million customers, is worth over $1 billion, and has paved the way for consumer genetics and personalized medicine.

Contrast those examples with more traditional strategic planning methods that use an inside-out approach. These approaches often start by examining the organization's performance, strengths, and weaknesses and then focus on beating the competition. Relatively little attention is paid to the broader macro environment and how it might create enormous new opportunities—or potential threats.

The goal is not to predict or control these underlying forces, but to become aware of signals that suggest a possible future becoming the inevitable present. It also allows leaders to better explore expansive questions such as: What's the most extreme outcome? What is inevitable? What are the "robust" moves that we should be taking regardless of which future unfolds? What should we be monitoring more closely? What conversations and new relationships would help inform how, when, and why the future might unfold in certain directions? And most importantly, how do you build this capability into your personal practice or learning and also this approach into the strategic conversations throughout your organization?

Shaping Potential Futures: Investing in Sustainable and Equitable Outcomes

Once you're able to see a variety of futures, how do you shape it toward the futures you want to bring to life?

In late December 2017, the MacArthur Foundation announced a historic $100 million grant to Sesame Workshop and the International Rescue Committee (IRC) to create the largest early intervention education program for young children displaced by conflict and instability in the Middle East.

Working together, these two unlikely partners pooled their unique strengths—Sesame Workshop's 50-year history of producing early childhood education programs and IRC's global network of foreign aid resources—to reduce the long-term impact of trauma on the nearly 30 million refugee children overlooked by other forms of humanitarian aid.

Thinking like a futurist, we know these children won't stay children forever—without a stable foundation and access to education, their future prospects may even be worse.

Both organizations believed providing refugee camps with high-quality, mobile educational resources would constitute the most meaningful shift in the lives and futures of this highly at-risk population, the region, and possibly the world.

According to Jeffrey Dunn, then President of Sesame Workshop: "These children are arguably the most vulnerable, and by improving their lives, we create a more stable and secure world for us all."[3]

But it doesn't take a $100 million dollar grant to be a future shaper. There are future shapers all around us—investing deeply in their communities to lift the prospects for all.

In the class I teach at Stanford, called "Inventing the Future," the capstone project asks student teams to debate the 50-year utopia and dystopia of an emerging technology, such as synthetic biology, the metaverse, or flying cars. Teams are asked to paint a vivid picture of society in that future through short videos that explore the implications of how the technology might play out. We also invite an expert from the field to come, share commentary, and ask questions about the team's thesis.

Unlike typical debates that judge the "winner" based on which team presented the strongest case, we ask the student groups to share what they learned from the other teams. What surprised them about the future they shared? What would have to be true for this future to unfold? What would help facilitate the more positive outcome? What would inoculate you from the future you'd like to avoid?

We want our students to practice what it feels like to reach and stretch toward the fantastical to expose potential risks and hidden benefits that short-term analysis might not reveal. In almost every debate, the expert guest walks away with new ideas and questions for their own research or industry. By asking unexpected questions, exploring adjacencies, or pursuing alternative pathways of potential downstream consequences and implications, we flex our capacity to shape new futures.

Share Futures That Make Us Feel

As leaders and future-shapers, learning how to share the future in compelling, engaging, and memorable ways is a critical skill. All too often, our polished projection-filled presentations on where the business should go generate enthusiasm but fail to get resources and funding to act on it.

For many years, Kyle Ne was executive director of Innovation for Lowe's Hardware. His job was to come up with bold ideas about how Lowe's could use emerging technology to drive growth and customer loyalty.

As an expert in behavioral science, Kyle had imaginative, inventive, future-shaping ideas, which he presented regularly to the executive board. But while Kyle received kudos for his foresight, he rarely got the collective buy-in to bring those ideas to life. Frustrated by this pattern, he changed course.

Kyle hired writers and illustrators from science fiction to collaborate on a graphic novel. He dreamed up scenarios that—no matter how far-fetched—led to faster, more efficient buying decisions, and customers who enjoyed the experience more. Included were AI-powered robots and VR headsets that let Lowe's shoppers visualize a remodel in advance.

After many failed attempts at getting traction and funding for his projects, Kyle's graphic novel started gaining attention. Within nine months, Lowe's flagship store in San Jose began greeting guests with an autonomous robot—the first in a string of innovations.[4] Soon after, Lowe's put the first 3D printer on the International Space Station, through a partnership with a startup called Made in Space.

Kyle used the power of story to bring the future to life. Not just any story—but a compelling one, complete with actual characters, plots, and vivid details.

Kyle also made his story visual and memorable. The images gave the ideas form and shape. This helped the executives see and feel the future through a shared experience. They didn't have to interpret words or promises—it was visualized in front of them.

Finally, Kyle's storytelling was exciting and accessible, allowing the executives to feel they were part of a new, visionary future. They could share the visual artifact widely with others, becoming advocates of the new possible.

We Can All Lead Like Futurists

Leading like a futurist is not a daunting, exclusive skillset that only a few can master. These practices and postures are available to all of us today. They can help us move from feeling that "the future is going to happen to me, and I don't know what to do" to a productive and proactive stance of agency and possibility.

Seeing, shaping, and sharing the future are ongoing learning and leadership practices designed to fuel clarity about our changing context, spark bold ideas and innovation, and prompt deep conversations and experiences that foster resilience and regeneration.

The future isn't some magical force that will descend on us, nor should it be designed by a chosen few. The future should be open for all of us to imagine—and build—together.

We can—and must be—the dreamers, the inventors, the artists, the creators, the pioneers, the shapers of our own tomorrows. The future needs that from us. And we owe it to the future.

Biography

Lisa Kay Solomon has been practicing and teaching futures thinking and design for nearly two decades. A bestselling author and dedicated educator, this chapter builds on her work teaching and running leadership programs on futures thinking at the Stanford d.school. In 2022, she was named to the Thinkers50 Radar list of up-and-coming thinkers whose ideas could make a positive difference in the world.

Notes

1. https://www.prospectivepsych.org/.
2. https://hbr.org/2013/05/the-corp-is-odds-future.
3. https://philanthropynewsdigest.org/news/macarthur-awards-100-million-to-sesame-workshop-irc.
4. Interviews with Kyle Nel. https://www.cnbc.com/2016/08/30/lowes-introduces-lowebot-a-new-autonomous-in-store-robot.html.

3

The Privilege of Leadership

A Constant in an Uncertain World

Sheree Atcheson

Privilege, according to the Merriam Webster dictionary definition is "a right or immunity granted as a peculiar benefit, advantage, or favor. Ultimately, a benefit given to specific groups and excluded from others."[1]

To many, privilege is a complicated topic, one that is precariously stepped over, full of nuances that are tricky to delve into, and therefore avoided altogether. For far too long, privilege conversations in the workplace have been boiled down to a simple "yes" or "no," 1 or 0. This binary approach erodes the difficult conversations required to traverse this space successfully, which would enable our leaders to recognize and rebalance our workplaces in very necessary ways.

Self-Awareness Is Key

Before we talk about rebalancing how we lead, let's talk about our own awareness of privilege. Privilege conversations can be complicated, but really, they don't need to be. The reason they're complicated is because people get defensive about honest facts regarding access (or the lack thereof). Suggesting someone is privileged is often viewed as a way to denounce or diminish their success, without recognizing that you can be successful and that privilege can, in many ways, have aided that success.

Just because you are privileged, no one is saying you haven't worked hard. What I am saying, however, is that due to certain factors like age, gender, ethnicity, socio-economic background, disability, sexual orientation, and so on, your journey may have been easier than those who have different obstacles.

I offer myself as an example. As a woman of color in industry in a senior leadership role, I am privileged. Likewise, as a senior woman of color in industry in a leadership role, I am underrepresented. Two things can be true at the same time.

The balance of being underrepresented yet privileged is not lost on me. I was adopted at three weeks old from Sri Lanka by a working-class Irish family. I grew up in rural Ireland (with my brother who is also adopted), where there were few other people of color. I faced extreme racism growing up, shaping my worldview. My parents ended up being disabled, so I grew up on free school meals.

But, despite these huge obstacles to overcome, because I was adopted, I was given access to opportunities that I simply couldn't have had in Sri Lanka. I was able to get grants to be the first in my family to go to university. I was able to find a career for myself, first as an engineer, and gain financial security. Until I did it, there was no generational wealth in my family. I have a name and accent which does not highlight that I am a woman of color, until you see my face, of course. Before that, you'd assume I was a white Irish woman.

Even with these privileges, however, I have faced bias at almost every stage of my career, primarily because of my gender, age, ethnicity, and my accent. People make assumptions about me and although I am thankful that I have been able to demolish them, I shouldn't have to. While I fit the profile of being underrepresented here in Europe, I've been back to Sri Lanka and found my biological family—and recognize that their decision to give me up for adoption has afforded me access to the many privileges I now have.

One of which is leadership.

The Weight of Leadership

The Merriam Webster dictionary definition of a leader is "a person who has commanding authority or influence."[2]

Think about that. Someone who has influence or authority—over other people. Someone whom others seek out for guidance, direction, and vision, creating a one-to-many relationship. For me, leadership is one of the biggest privileges any of us can have. When we have the responsibility of making decisions which affect other people, we must ensure that our decisions are not riddled with biases, that they consider all different perspectives before implementation and delivery and that we have not relied heavily on assumption over data. We must be pro-active instead of reactive.

There are fewer leaders in the world than there are employees or people following those leaders' direction. To me, that is why leadership is such a privilege. Being a leader means that ultimately, we are listened to—and we actively know this when we speak. We know that when we decide to share our ideas or vision, that people will spend time digesting what we say. For us, that is usually a certainty. That's not to say that some leaders aren't listened to more than others. It's impossible, and frankly facetious, to discount the lens of diversity on leadership.

For example, in the Fortune 500 '22 list, 158 CEOs and CFOs at the companies studied are female or racially or ethnically diverse (or both), nearly double the number in the 2012 report (86). In 2022, 7.3% of sitting CEOs and 16% of CFOs were women, up from 3.5% and 9.7%, respectively, a decade ago. Some 10.7% of sitting CEOs and 10.9% of CFOs were racially or ethnically diverse, up from 5.4% and 3.6%, respectively, a decade ago. Overall, 88.8% of CEOs, CFOs, and COOs in the 2022 report are Caucasian, and 88.1% are men.[3]

So, while, yes, all these people share the privilege of leadership, there are clear differences in representation. What's important to note here is that those in majority demographics are listened to differently to those in minority demographics. Consider the difficulty of not only sharing the different opinions of those not commonly represented in these rooms, but also being the person most likely to provide friction before decision-making. The minority demographics leader has to deal with being the contrarian who also bursts echo chambers by sharing differing opinions that cause disruption. In my view, this is a good thing! However, it means people may treat you negatively because of a potential "them and us" mentality.'

Affinity bias affects how and who we listen to, and we are more likely to listen to those who are like us than those who are not. Having diversity in the room is great, but if those same people are not listened to or given the same opportunities to speak, then this is fruitless and pointless.

A great way to determine if you're listening to everyone equally is to think about how you listen to them. When someone speaks, are you listening to what they say, taking a moment to digest their views and insights, and then responding? Or have you already decided what you're going to say before they've finished, so really, you're simply waiting for your turn to speak?

Think about the impact on those around us when we do this. It's not inclusive, nor is it welcoming. I also want you to think harder about who we listen to in either of these ways and why.

If we listen to most leaders in the first way, and most leaders fall into majority demographics, then does that mean we inadvertently create a bias to actively listening to this group of people versus others?

Given that most of those in leadership roles are not from underrepresented groups, many of us will not have the opportunity to listen to them as peers. And if we deem leaders as worthy of listening to and everyone else as not, then we create a clear bias toward which groups we define as "important" enough to give our consideration to. This is where we must really challenge how we listen to all people, as we sit with the privilege of leadership. Otherwise, we make vast and large decisions in echo chambers, and that does not serve society well because society is not a monolithic group.

Embedding Friction Before Decision-Making

As leaders, we will make decisions throughout our tenures, whether that is hiring, promotion, business growth, or strategy decisions. In many environments we work in, we're expected to move at pace, because at the end of the day, time is money and we're expected to use our expertise to provide logic and reasoning to why we choose X over Y.

Realistically, many of us share our leadership remits with like-minded people—whether that is because of our background, our leadership styles, our personality types, or any other reason. This can mean we make decisions that follow the path of least resistance—consciously or unconsciously we choose the smoothest way. Now, this might sound fine, but decisions made without friction mean we're working in echo chambers—environments with groupthink and more agreement than disagreement.

No one wants an environment where everyone disagrees all the time, but what we should aim for is embracing friction before decision-making. To embed this into your processes:

- **Ensure diversity of perspectives is welcomed, before sign-off or roll out:** Seek different perspectives that may not be in the room through user-groups, employee surveys or having connections to those from marginalized groups who may be just below the leadership level.
- **For large-scale decisions, create user-personas** (or think about the way the decision may affect different groups of people through creating characters): This will enable a more rigorous sign-off process, instead of assuming something will work for group X because it works for group Y.
- **Slow down:** This is the hardest thing to do, but sometimes, taking just a minute to really assess our choices helps. Asking ourselves (or asking the room) "why" five times can help get to the root of our choice, which takes us away from being unbalanced or unfair.

Leadership Will Always Be Necessary: Let's Make It Equitable

Organizations will always require leadership. People with experience to fulfill this role will be a necessity and those people typically come from an operational background within the very teams they will now lead. I want you to think about how the leadership we have and instill now will shape the leaders we have in the future. Take a step back and recognize that much of this is bigger than any of us as individuals.

To do this:

- **Share growth opportunities fairly:** For us to have an array of talent from different backgrounds in the future, we must have an array of people at the level just below leadership. The only way to achieve that is for people of all backgrounds to have the opportunity to showcase their growth and success through difficult assignments. Do not always assign these projects to your usual "safe pair of hands," but rather, understand who has had the opportunity and more importantly, who hasn't, and go from there. We cannot have equitable environments if some people are given more opportunities than others.

- **Dissect data across groups, embedding intersectionality:** Data is key because it does not lie. Gather people analytics on how management supports belonging, reward, and so on. Ensure you do not take a broad-stroke view, but rather, delve into these analytics across gender, gender x seniority, and any other marginalized groups you may have data on.

- **Be willing to be wrong:** As leaders, it's easy for us to assume what we decide is immediately correct, but that doesn't leave room for new, fresh thinkers or ideas to step forward and share.

Manifesting of Privilege: One of Life's Constants

Privilege does not disappear or dissipate. It will always be there, and it will be embedded in how our processes work (or don't work) and how we make decisions. Wouldn't it be wonderful if, instead of leaving it to stagnate, we could do something meaningful with it?

That requires that we, as leaders, recognize our own privilege and how it affects our ways of thinking so that when we finish doing this work (whatever it may be), we can honestly say we have left things better than we found them.

Biography

Sheree Atcheson is one of the UK's Most Influential Women in Tech and an international multi-award winner for her services to diversity and inclusion in industry. She is the author of *Demanding More*, a book which aims to teach readers about how deliberate exclusion has been in systems and society, so they can be purposefully and deliberately inclusive moving forward. In 2022, she was named to the Thinkers50 Radar list of up-and-coming thinkers whose ideas could make a positive difference in the world.

Notes

1. https://www.merriam-webster.com/dictionary/leader/privilege.
2. https://www.merriam-webster.com/dictionary/leader.
3. https://static1.squarespace.com/static/62164a05607c3e5978f251ec/t/62ffa2444929874d096206be/1660920447417/Crist+Kolder+2022+Summer+V+Report.

4

Leading from the Future (Not the Past)

Terence Mauri

If leaders consider "the one thing they could do differently today to help their organization be future prepared," where would they start? As leaders respond to remote and hybrid work models, humans and machines, workforce ecosystems, and talent marketplaces, embedding future-focused leadership is the best way to say goodbye to the status quo, make trust leaps into the future and turn uncertainty into a tailwind for laser-like focus and strategic courage.

Change used to happen as a breeze. Now it feels like a category-5 typhoon. With economic headwinds and market dislocation an everyday reality, the best solution is to activate future-focused leadership that empowers workers to turn foresight into insight and emerging trends into new pathways for growth, meaning, and value creation. Which is worse? (1) We saw the trends coming, or (2) We saw the trends coming and didn't act. One of the clearest signs of future-focused leadership is reframing and rethinking your assumptions about what stays, what changes, and what goes. This matters because the complexity of issues is outstripping our human capacity to respond—leading to a high leadership tax (less time to focus on value creation, productivity, and growth) and record levels of overload, distraction, and risk of burnout.

Future-focused leadership is defined as a way of leading and managing that inspires workers to challenge the status quo and unlearn the always-done ways that no longer work. Too often, we value knowing above learning and prioritize doing over thinking. Leaders who care about leading from the future go big on better sense-making and choice-making, starting with asking deeply human-centric questions.

- Do we practice future-focused leadership?
- Do we minimize or maximize freedom and responsibility?
- Do we commodify or humanize the work experience?
- Do we obsess over values, not just metrics?
- Do we make the invisible visceral?
- Do we enable wise choices, not just the fastest?
- Do we bind trust to freedom and responsibility?
- Do we nurture mindfulness?
- Do we strengthen existing human brilliance?

To lead from the future, leaders should reject "present forward" ways of thinking and taken-for-granted norms that simply extend existing assumptions, mental maps, and talent frameworks to the future. This leadership style worked well in a complicated world (linear, predictable, and rules-based) but is less relevant for thriving in a complex world (non-linear, unpredictable, and fluid). A failure to reimagine is a failure of leadership. Instead, leaders should avoid empty slogans and go big on co-creation, distributed trust, and the courage to turn volatility into value. Companies such as Orsted, DBS, Hermès, Ocado, and Estée Lauder champion this future-focused principle by sharpening their bold agenda for culture, people, and talent, and building profitable growth engines despite their complex legacy businesses.

This means:

- context over control;
- autonomy over rules;
- speaking up over silence;

- career agility over career ladders;
- iterative growth mindsets over bureaucratic fixed ones;
- simplicity over complexity.

Future-focused leaders care about the Human Agenda: return on intelligence, return on energy, and return on integrity not just return on investment. They are redesigning skills and workflows that are future-focused and match talent to value in ways that make workers feel more alive and empowered. While workers all over the world are rethinking their purpose at work, the rules and styles of today's leaders have dramatically evolved.

Operating at the edge of uncertainty, framing becomes a skill. Now the only certainty is uncertainty. Leaders should strengthen their context-setting, culture-setting, talent-setting, and pace-setting capabilities to ensure wise and focused alignment with their top strategic priorities. Execution certainty matters too. Hack Future Lab's research shows that only 1 in 4 workers knows more than three of the company's top five strategic priorities, creating a big gap between aspiration and action.

In Futures, We Grow

As global growth stalls and organizations struggle to retain top talent, future-focused leadership is a source of resilience and growth. Leaders who want to outpace the multiplying and overlapping forces of disruption and strengthen human brilliance should reflect on whether their existing cultures, structures, and work models are built for future-focused leadership or conformity-focused leadership. Conformity-focused leadership is a way of leading that deters workers from challenging the status quo. It's silence over speaking up, fear over freedom and "fake" empowerment over active decision-making whereby workers have the job title but not the power or autonomy to make decisions that matter. It demands deference and downgrades human potential.

Research by Hack Future Lab shows that the number one reason why workers quit, after money, is a lack of internal growth opportunities and 79% of workers do not think their current employer offers long-term, growth-led opportunities. As workforce turnover continues to surge and organizations struggle to retain talent, leaders must make future-focused leadership a priority if they're aiming to boost performance, engagement, and retention.

Leading from the future is always less risky than a weak strategy or weak leadership. A future-focused leader models the curiosity to learn and the courage to unlearn. Learning helps you evolve, and unlearning helps you keep up as the world evolves.

Future-focused leaders activate enterprise-wide mindsets and behaviors such as:

- **The curiosity to learn:** The gap between what you know and what you want to know.
- **The courage to unlearn:** As the rate of change accelerates, you must unlearn the always-done ways.
- **The clarity to focus:** Pay attention to attention and focus on deep leadership (high impact) more than shallow leadership (low impact).
- **The conviction to decide:** High-velocity decisions that shape the future and say goodbye to the status quo.
- **The care to co-create:** High safety and high diversity teams that belong, contribute, challenge, and show high-risk tolerance for iterating and experimenting.

Hack Future Lab took the pulse of 1,000 leaders globally. An overwhelming 84% agreed that future-focused leadership is critical for business success and 68% agreed that it is the best way to boost contribution, engagement, and retention. The bad news was that more than half the group reported that conformity-focused leadership was the norm and was not even on the C-suite's agenda as a challenge to be tackled. The bottom line is that future-focused leadership is seen as incredibly important but is mismanaged and undervalued in most organizations.

New Beginnings

Many leaders are stuck between the certainties of the past and the unknowns of the future. I believe that a change in perspective is required to unlock the huge benefits of future-focused leadership because your current perceptions are grounded in your past assumptions. Re-perception—the ability to see, hear, or become aware of something new in existing information and notice the blind spots that we are blind to—is at the heart of unlearning and is crucial for sustaining future-focused leadership for the long term. To help leaders do so, it is worth asking several questions: What is unlearning and how do you sustain it for the long term? What are the mindset shifts, assumptions, and risks for this journey?

Unlearning is a form of future readiness and an accelerant for future-focused leadership. At its core, unlearning is a leader's capacity to rethink assumptions and update mental maps and behaviors to avoid inertia or culture and transformation drift. When the ratio of assumptions to knowledge is high and the operating environment is volatile, the best way of staying relevant is to build platforms of unlearning where workers have the psychological safety to eliminate old ways of working and challenge outdated assumptions and leadership behaviors that (1) no longer serve the purpose, and (2) destroy value.

Hack Future Lab's research shows that 70% of workers believe their voice doesn't matter at work. That's a sad indictment of the health of leadership today and another reason why leaders should not waste the biggest unlearning moment in their lifetimes. The case for unlearning is urgent and timely and sits at the heart of activating future-focused leadership because today's leadership challenges can't be solved with yesterday's thinking.

The Wisdom Gap

One of the biggest leadership paradoxes of our time is that technology changes fast but humans don't. Leaders are trapped in a wisdom gap with the complexities of runaway technology outstripping our human brains' capacity to make sense of it all (e.g., consider the processing power of a computer chip has increased over a trillion times). And while technology isn't the only reason, runaway technology is rapidly widening the wisdom gap even further, leading to cultural and structural stupidity. Data isn't the new oil. Wisdom is the new oil. For example, the number of words in the US Tax Code has increased from 400,000 to 4 million in the last 20 years, highlighting a human bias toward bureaucratic bloat and adding complexity to complexity. Excess bureaucracy is a tax on human potential and excess complexity is a tax on shaping the future.

Hack Future Lab embarked on a research initiative to understand how a select few companies demonstrate future-focused leadership, transforming their businesses and illuminating the way forward for others. Most leaders get trapped in the baseline fallacy trap which is the idea that the current business model and way of leading are a low risk bet until that isn't true, at which point it's probably too late to do anything about it. But now the half-life of advantage has shrunk to just one year. That means that long-term sustainable success becomes very hard and very rare and requires the twin demands of leading for today while transforming for tomorrow. Leaders who want to avoid getting trapped by strong convictions and the always-done ways can stay on top by practicing deliberate future-focused leadership that is an alchemy of high learning orientation, exploring early to exploit know-how sooner, and wise and fast decision-making.

Pfizer is known for its nine-month race to make the impossible possible by creating the first Covid-19 vaccine in the world. What you may not know is that the company is on a mission to harness volatility as a tailwind to lead from the future by activating future-focused mindsets across the 79,000-person enterprise (act at the speed of science, crush bureaucracy, believe in the purpose, and trust one another) and bringing values to life every day (courage, equity, excellence, and joy at work). Pfizer CEO Albert Bourla, a provocateur of future-focused leadership, knows that to change the game you must make game-changing moves:

- Reskilling, cross-skilling, and upskilling all employees with future-fit skills by 2025.
- Scaling cultures of curiosity based on high-risk tolerance for experimentation.
- Reframing failure as a platform that welcomes ideas to improve the status quo.
- Role-modeling and sharing stories of unlearning the "always-done ways" through reflection, feed-forward, recognition, and celebration.

The #1 takeaway is that when the future arrives faster than ever before, not taking a risk is the risk. Leaders always overestimate the risk of trying something new and underestimate the risk of standing still. The best leaders don't just survive a crisis. They use it as a platform to get smarter, more flexible, and more focused.

Future-Focused, We Grow

Workers want to thrive in human-led, tech-enabled cultures offering dynamic portfolios of reinvention that combine meaning, education, and skills over a lifetime, and scale what makes them more human: radiate purpose, inclusivity at scale, belonging, and deep work that workers love. Data at the Mayo Clinic suggests that if less than 20% of your work consists of things you love to do, you are more than 6.7x more likely to suffer from burnout (cognitive and emotional burnout) or "bore out," e.g., cognitive underload.

To unlock future-focused leadership in your organization, there are three bold moves to consider (Figure 4.1):

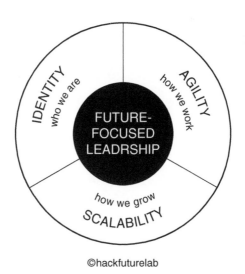

©hackfuturelab

Figure 4.1 Future-focused leadership.
Source: Hack Future Lab.

1. **Who we are (Identity):** Sharpen the purpose and trust agenda, e.g., treat culture like a product (embrace perpetual beta) and go big on radiating purpose, values as an accelerant and trust safety (safety to speak up, safety to challenge, and safety to be vulnerable).

2. **How we work (Agility):** Replace fake empowerment with context over control, distributed trust and directly responsible individuals (DRI), e.g., help workers understand different decision types from big-bet decisions to cross-cutting and delegated decisions.

3. **How we grow (Scalability):** Scale for long-term value (LTV) and rethink human capability stacks around talent to value creation, e.g., leverage AI-powered talent marketplaces that break down silos and increase internal growth and mobility opportunities.

Future-focused leaders such as Mastercard, Lululemon, and Microsoft are pioneers at making bold moves around identity, agility, and scalability. For example, they have all committed to making the invisible visceral by leading the enterprise together, empowering others to make decisions, driving their organizations outside their comfort zones, championing the future, and, perhaps most importantly, not limiting their challenges but challenging their limits. The outcome is a bold dividend, meaning future-focused leaders are 2.2× more likely to outperform their peers, 3× more likely to innovate, and 5× more likely to have high execution certainty.

Uncertain Times Require Future-Makers

To lead from the future, leaders must nurture their relationship with the unknown. Every organization starts as an act of imagination but to sustain vitality for the long term requires reimagination, which is the human force that can push through inertia to create a better future. The disruptive trends that threaten to upend and reshape every vertical over the next five years—disintermediation in the supply chains, erosion of traditional economies of scale advantages, and more companies dying younger—will only accelerate. The question is: as leaders, how do you capitalize on the disruptive forces of the last few years and shape future-focused leadership with bold intentionality?

Biography

Terence Mauri is the founder of the global management think tank Hack Future Lab, an entrepreneur mentor in residence at M.I.T. and London Business School, and an Adjunct Professor at IE Business School. He is the author of *The 3D Leader: Take Your Leadership to the Next Dimension*. In 2019, he was named to the Thinkers50 Radar list of up-and-coming thinkers whose ideas could make a positive difference in the world.

5

Toward Uncertainty Ability

Leading Self and Others to Possibility Beyond the Unknown

Nathan Furr and
Susannah Harmon Furr

In the December 2008 *McKinsey Quarterly*, authors Lowell Bryan and Diana Farrell[1] penned a wise treatment from the depths of a financial crisis that still holds insight for our current global landscape of steadily increasing uncertainty. Their sobering article gets it right from the first paragraphs—there is a paradoxical nature of uncertainty—that it is both the birthplace of "extraordinary opportunities" *and* of "impulsive, uncoordinated, and ultimately ineffective responses." And while they offer a compelling triumvirate of skills for the effective navigation of uncertainty within organizations (more flexible, more aware, more resilient), they quickly finish their article by directing the responsibility at leaders: "The future will belong to companies *whose senior executives remain calm.*"

Far from being tongue in cheek, it's true. Leaders and organizations need to develop an ability to face uncertainty. Serial entrepreneur and CEO Sam Yagan agrees: "The single biggest predictor of executive success is how you deal with ambiguity."[2] Panic, anxiety, and rumination are sure-fire ways to derail effective navigation of any type of uncertainty but remaining calm isn't natural when facing the unknown. Humans are wired to avoid uncertainty at all costs. Numerous studies in the fields of evolutionary science, neuroscience, and psychology have shown that humans, quite reasonably, are wired for survival; and anything unfamiliar, unknown, or uncertain registers as dangerous. Luckily, research in the domains of ambiguity tolerance, uncertainty avoidance, and resilience all underscore that we can learn to face uncertainty well. Still, attempts to explain *how* have been either too vague or too new age to serve as a robust guide with actionable tools for personal and organizational application.

If individuals are the ones responsible for getting their companies to the extraordinary opportunities beyond uncertainty, we need a framework that speaks to the human inside the manager first. To that end, we have been talking with innovators, entrepreneurs, creatives, artists, scientists, and leaders, i.e., people who have repeatedly experienced the possibility waiting just beyond the unknown and who have made peace with the disquieting emotions and setbacks that are a natural part of the progression toward any discovery. The main takeaway of these conversations was clear: there is an upside to uncertainty. It is quite simply the portal to every innovation, change, and transformation we celebrate but often absorb as familiar facts as soon as they are made certain to us.

Bolstered by that extremely hopeful reality, that uncertainty and possibility are just two sides of the same coin, in our book, *The Upside of Uncertainty*, we created a framework that aims to help individuals and then, naturally, the companies they inhabit.[3] Our interviews and research presented in that book led us to pinpoint more than 40 tools that uncertainty-thriving individuals regularly invoke when facing the unknown. To facilitate their remembrance and use, we group them in four categories situated around a "first aid cross for uncertainty." When individuals learn about and practice the tools that *reframe*, *prime*, *do*, and *sustain* their forays with uncertainty, they will increase what we naturally call their "uncertainty ability"—the skill to navigate unknowns both planned (such as starting a new venture or leaving a job) and unplanned (such as losing a job, experiencing a health crisis, or going through a relationship breakdown).

Reframing

Based on a long tradition of study started by Daniel Kahneman and Amos Tversky, we know that humans are gain-seeking and loss-averse. This means the way we frame, or describe, something ultimately impacts how we think, decide, and act. When things are framed as impossible, dangerous, or threatening in any way we will experience a strong aversion toward that thing—even if it's good for us because with that frame it is registering as a source of impending loss. However, when that same thing is reframed as possible, beneficial, and valuable we are more likely to give it a go—in spite of the obstacles— and in some cases we might even eagerly seek it because we are considering it in terms of what we might gain.

One of the most empowering reframe tools encourages seeking an "adjacent possible," a term taken from biology to explain a sort of "shadow future hovering at the edge of things." When facing uncertainty, it can be tempting to force and control outcomes that have worked before or even prematurely take a decision when a better outcome might be just around the corner waiting to be recognized. To encourage you to consider how many adjacent possibles there are, we share a beautiful expansive quote by the late poet and philosopher John O'Donohue:

> Possibilities are always more interesting than facts. We shouldn't frown on fact, but our world is congested with them. But for every fact that becomes a fact, there are seven, eight, maybe five hundred possibilities hanging around in the background that didn't make it in to the place where they could be elected and realised as the actual fact.[4]

An example of this in action is found in the beautiful work of marine biologist, Dr. Ayana Johnson, who is facing climate crisis with a radically optimistic adjacent possible: "what if we get this right?"

She roots this question in her deep love of all the joyful aspects of Earth life that she hopes we could figure out how to hold onto. Reframing this dire situation not in terms of the extinction and grave existential worry (which she agrees are real) but in terms of the good-will and love we have for this planet and each other, provides a power-ful way forward that is way more energizing than the stressful, overwhelming varieties that leave many of us confused about how to even start digging ourselves out of the carbon footprints we can't ever hope to pay back. Interestingly, most experts working on this issue aren't used to looking at this from that lens. What if we get this right is a fantastic question for any uncertain journey, and one we have started saying to each other when we are facing any tricky situation.

Priming

Priming refers to preliminary behaviors we may be tempted to skip that positively impact the experience and quality of the activity we are going to engage in next (i.e., priming an engine, priming a wall when painting, or priming a water pump all determine the effectiveness of the final outcome). The goal isn't to take on every uncertainty beckon-ing or threatening you, and when the level of uncertainty you are facing is particularly high, you should opt out of optional uncertainties where possible. But when uncertainty is not optional or required to achieve your goals, priming is about preparing yourself to face it well. Tools in this category involve sense-making steps around self-knowledge, such as graphing your personal risk affinity and aversion zones on a risk-o-meter, situational-knowledge, such as elucidating which resources you have and which constraints you face, and self-protection, such as uncertainty balancers, which provide an oasis of comfort and certainty.

Uncertainty balancers can be any comforting habit, routine, or people you can rely on to instill certainty, to offset the morass of uncer-tainty you are facing to help you avoid maladaptive balancers (work-aholism, addiction, negative individuals) that ultimately sabotage your ability to find the possibility you are seeking. Our interviews revealed over and over that individuals who thrive under uncertainty use mundane uncertainty balancers, such as carrying their own favorite breakfast with them and staying in the exact same hotel room or automating their wardrobes. While friends, partners, and life coaches tended to be the most critical source of balance, creating weekly rituals can be extremely powerful uncertainty balancers for teams, such as the weekly "highs and lows" sharing sessions with drinks after which have been ranked as the most helpful office meeting at EVBox, an electric charging start-up in Paris. *New York Times* bestselling author Bessel van der Kolk doesn't like to equate uncertainty with trauma, as the stress it creates often resolves when it's over, but he does warn that "most self-destructive behaviours started out as strategies for self-protection." [5] One of Nathan's colleagues at INSEAD treats himself to peanut butter and jelly sandwiches on days he knows are going to be challenging, something about the comforting sandwich helps him rally. *Uncertainty balancers: you can't have too many.*

Doing

Obviously, the best way out of uncertainty is to engage with it and take some decisive action. However, forcing outcomes or stubbornly clinging to what's worked under previous scenarios of certainty will likely fizzle out and fall flat. Having reframed and primed, individuals facing uncertainty are more likely to do things like calm Zen warriors: thoughtfully, incrementally, wisely. The darn reality is that most efforts will require bricolage, small steps, pivots, and cognitive flexibility . . . and as many as 10,000 shots (all refer to specific tools in the Do toolkit from our book, *The Upside of Uncertainty*).[6] Our favorite *doers* under uncertainty understood something counter-intuitive about what progress looks like, choosing to make decisions led by their internal values rather than external-based metrics or goals.

Brian Chesky, CEO of Airbnb, demonstrated this brilliantly during the pandemic, when the business dropped 80% in eight weeks:

> The hardest thing to manage in a crisis isn't your company—it's your own thoughts. As a leader, you could think all is doomed. You can ask, 'Why me?' You can get paralyzed. Or, you can tell

yourself, 'This is my defining moment, and it will leave indelible marks.' Then you can be optimistic—not with blind optimism but optimism rooted in facts that give you hope of getting out of the situation. If you can project that confidence, abide by your principles, and act quickly, then you can navigate out of the crisis like a captain on a ship that is starting to take on water.[7]

When layoffs were required, he based all decisions on his value to honor those employees and be as generous as possible. He asked himself how could he do *more* for those folks than what was expected? The answer was a brilliant combination of a year of healthcare coverage for US employees, the gift of their company laptops, increasing their likelihood of finding new jobs by creating an alumni directory, asking CEOs to hire from his talented pool, and being authentic in his letter wherein he expressed his love. He knew it might come off as cheesy, but he said it was an authentic emotion as he felt extremely responsible for the decision and wanted to champion the gifts they had given his company.

When we face uncertainty from this values-mindset, often our way forward is made clear. Danish author and tech entrepreneur, David Heinemeier Hansson claims that leading a company, a project, a life based on values is the only way to not fail under uncertainty.[8]

Sustaining

Uncertainty almost always unfolds differently than we thought and sometimes it gets worse before it gets better. Whether you call it failure or learning what doesn't work is an example of a reframe made for moments when setbacks and obstacles weigh heavily on you. Sustaining tools are fantastic for getting you back on the horse and they fall into three categories: (1) *emotional hygiene* (consistent and skillful care of our emotional "bodies"); (2) *reality check* (using our reasoning minds to cut through the gloom of negative or naïve stories with as little bias and anxiety as possible); and (3) *magic* (the sudden leaps of insight, the serendipitous encounters, the fortuitous events that we can't take credit for but we can put ourselves in situations where they are more likely to occur).

One interesting reality check tool teaches us to see our competitors as collaborators rather than fear their ability to overtake us. Viewed from that lens, competitors can be "reframed" as the best people who will inspire us to do our best work. Cyclists Jacques Anquetil and Raymond Poulidor raced like madmen up and down the steep 10 km terrain of the Puy du Dôme segment in the 1964 Tour de France and later remembered it as the hardest race they ever rode. They were enjoying the experience of mastery and thrilled the onlookers with their extreme skill and speed with unyielding tenacity. If we see competitors or critics of our work as there to help us get better, a more interesting game ensues. Recently, a humdrum review of *The Upside of Uncertainty* wherein we share this entire toolkit was summarized as being too focused on outliers and narrow visions of success, which gutted us because one of our main objectives with the book was that it should be exactly the opposite. When we reached out to the reviewer and started a conversation, we found a friend and potential collaborator on future projects. It turned out that we share so much and long for business books that will champion underdogs and a new vision of success. While we were encouraged to "bury" the less-than-rave review, the reality check of creative competition reminded us to engage with our "competitor" and enlarge the possible outcomes.

These tools require regular practice at a personal level to become familiar, useful, and, hopefully one day, instinctual. Managers who envision being "calm" in the face of uncertainty can support others only after they have mustered the courage to go for mastery of these tools. Then, how naturally it will be to dignify their teams by giving them opportunities and encouragement to learn and practice these calm-enhancing tools as well.

Bryan and Farrell warned of what happens when calm isn't found: "Economies everywhere stagnate; overregulation and fear keep the global credit and capital markets closed. Trade and capital flows continue to decline for years as globalization goes into reverse, and the psychology of nations becomes much more defensive and nationalistic."[9] Clearly, we need a competency for uncertainty more than ever. But don't fret. Instead ask yourself, what if we get uncertainty right?

Biographies

Nathan Furr is Professor of Strategy at INSEAD in Paris and a recognized expert in the fields of innovation and technology strategy. His bestselling books include *The Innovator's Method*, *Leading Transformation*, *Innovation Capital*, and *The Upside of Uncertainty*. In 2019, he was shortlisted for Thinkers50 Distinguished Achievement Award for Innovation.

Susannah Harmon Furr is an entrepreneur, designer, art historian, and contrarian, based in Paris. She founded a women's clothing line inspired by her research on the intricate embroidery Dutch women found the time to painstakingly render on their otherwise unadorned uniforms—details often invisible to all but the wearer. She leads well-being retreats for individuals and teams and is a co-author of *The Upside of Uncertainty*.

Notes

1. Lowell Bryan and Diana Farrell, "Leading Through Uncertainty," *McKinsey Quarterly*, December (2008). https://www.mckinsey.com/capabilities/strategy-and-corporate-finance/our-insights/leading-through-uncertainty.
2. Sam Yagan, interview with Nathan Furr, May 21, 2020.
3. Nathan Furr and Susannah Harmon Furr, *The Upside of Uncertainty* (Boston: Harvard Business Review Press, 2022).
4. John O'Donohue, in conversation with John Quinn, *Walking in Wonder: Eternal Wisdom for a Modern World* (New York: Convergent, 2015).
5. Bessel van der Kolk, *The Body Keeps the Score: Brain, Mind, and Body in the Healing f Trauma* (New York: Penguin Books, 2015), p. 333.
6. Furr and Harmon Furr, *The Upside of Uncertainty*, op. cit.
7. James Manyika, "The 21st-Century Corporation: A Conversation with Bryan Chesky of Airbnb," Inside the Strategy Room podcast, McKinsey, July 23 2021. https://www.mckinsey.com/capabilities/strategy-and-corporate-finance/our-insights/the-21st-century-corporation-a-conversation-with-brian-chesky-of-airbnb.
8. David Heinemeier Hansson, interview with Nathan Furr and Susannah Harmon Furr.
9. Bryan and Farrell, op. cit.

Transformational Leadership

6

Leading with the Head and Heart

The Modern Leader Our World Needs Today

Kirstin Ferguson

This century, and even more recently through the pandemic, our notion of leadership has been turned on its head. No longer do we expect or want our leaders to be wise, heroic figureheads with decades of experience and who may have inherited their place in the world.

Our world needs modern leaders who recognize leadership itself is the privilege and not for the privileged few.

Just as our personal histories—including our origin stories, educational background, gender, sexuality, disabilities—define our individual leadership, so too does the history of who we have celebrated as leaders in the past. The idea that only some men were entitled to lead has driven our views of leadership for the past two centuries. Nineteenth-century Scottish historian, essayist, and philosopher Thomas Carlyle's Great Man theory rested on the assumption that all great leaders are born with certain traits allowing them to lead by instinct and to wield authority and power. So unique were the traits these men were born with, and so strong their power to inspire, they deserved to lead; the world needed such great men at the helm.

It has only been in recent years we have ushered in a new era of leadership recognizing leaders must lead from both the head and the heart. Corporate leaders like Satya Nadella, Marc Benioff, the late Arne Sorenson, along with former New Zealand's Prime Minister Jacinda Ardern and Ukraine's President Volodymyr Zelensky, all represent a new style of leadership on the world stage. They represent a new model of head and heart leadership for us all.

Modern Leaders Among Us

There is now widespread recognition that simply managing people to undertake tasks is not leadership. We seek leaders who set aside personal interest for the benefit of others, and who recognize humility is required to focus on the needs and aspirations of those they lead, rather than themselves. Authentic leaders are in demand; leaders with a growth mindset and the self-awareness to accurately assess their limitations and treat those they lead with respect.

As impressive as the leadership of Nadella, Benioff, Sorenson, Ardern, and Zelensky may be, they are still figures with official positions of power. What is equally important to remember when we think of modern leaders is that they lead among us every day. Modern leadership is not limited to a hierarchical position, as traditional leadership models of the past might have emphasized. If we continue to define leadership in a traditional hierarchical sense, then we continue to exclude, rather than include most people who are leading in their lives and workplaces.

Such a narrow definition of leaders ignores the informal leaders in our organizations who may not have formal authority but who are looked to by those they work with to guide the way. It ignores nurses who may not have direct reports, in the traditional sense, but who lead through the care and wellbeing they offer their patients. It ignores parents raising their families and it ignores leaders of ideas like activist Greta Thunberg who demonstrated leadership the moment she had a cause to believe in and decided to act.

Traditional views of leadership also ignore leaders of movements such as #MeToo and #Black Lives Matter. The co-creators of #Black Lives Matter include three Black women, two whom identify as queer and one who is an immigrant; modern leaders who through history have been forced to lead at the margins as we focused on celebrating heroic, generally male, leaders of the past.

The Eight Attributes of a Head and Heart Leader

Using quantitative research and academic literature, I have identified the eight leadership attributes for a modern, head and heart leader.

Thinking about the head and heart as a metaphor is not new. Plato first suggested the head as the source of rational wisdom, and the heart as the source of passion. The simple term "head and heart" has a long history and is a concept deeply embedded in Western culture.

I began by investigating the existing literature to identify those leadership concepts most frequently associated with leaders who are seen as highly capable and effective, as well as emotionally intelligent and able to build strong relationships.

Before confirming the eight attributes, the validity of each attribute was empirically tested in conjunction with Professor Lisa Bradley at the Queensland University of Technology (QUT) Business School. This validation process led to the development of the Head & Heart Leader Scale™.

You can read more about the Head & Heart Leader Scale™ in *Head & Heart: The Art of Modern Leadership,*[1] including information on the sample group, methodology, means, reliabilities, and correlations for the eight head and heart attributes. You can also complete the scale yourself by visiting www.headheartleader.com.

Head-Based Leadership Attributes

When we think of leading with our "head," I am referring to the cognitive, decision-making part of our brain. When we lead with our head we can analyze complex data, weigh up risks and opportunities, create business strategies, or write policies. Our head loves to focus on the tangible, find patterns, and think about what can be measured and reviewed. It is a safe place for many of us because we can see, feel, and touch the work we produce and there is no doubt capability and technical proficiency are incredibly important. Without the skills our rational brain affords us, we would never be able to fulfill what is required of us as a leader.

Through my research, I identified four attributes of leading with our "head" all modern leaders can call upon when needed:

- **Curiosity:** We have a genuine thirst to fill gaps in our knowledge, we acknowledge and accept that we do not know everything. We seek to challenge assumptions and rethink what we thought we knew.
- **Wisdom:** We use wisdom to assess what is known and unknown, weigh up risk and reward, search for data or evidence, and then assess the best possible path forward.
- **Perspective:** We lead with perspective in order to "read the room" in order to understand the culture, industry, environment or context we are leading in and make decisions on the best path to take to enable the best possible outcome for all.
- **Capability:** We build capability through having a growth mindset and leading with capability allows us to develop others to have a growth mindset too.

Heart-Based Leadership Attributes

Emotions have always influenced and impacted our decisions since humans are not, and never have been, automatons. Our heart, in a metaphorical sense, is where we process our emotions, feel a connection with others, and develop our values.

Leading with the "heart" is just as important for a modern leader as leading with our heads and refers to how we view, and are viewed, by the world. The output of leading with our "heart" may be more difficult to see and measure than that produced by our "heads" but is equally important and impacts the way we interact and relate to others.

Through my research, I identified four attributes of leading with our "heart" all modern leaders can call upon when needed:

- **Humility:** We are willing to seek out the contributions of others, accept some things are beyond our control, and we can withstand the temptation to prove our own knowledge or need to be "the smartest person in the room."
- **Self-awareness:** We have a high level of insight into our character, abilities, and limitations. We are aware of the impact we have on those around us and adapt our leadership as required.
- **Courage:** We can make decisions we believe are the right thing to do, even in the face of pressure from others not to do so. We create psychologically safe cultures where others feel able to speak up as well.
- **Empathy:** We can put ourselves in the shoes of others without taking on others' feelings ourselves. We can willingly, authentically, and respectfully listen and engage with diverse points of view and recognize it is in those differences where value lies.

The Art of Modern Leadership

The art of being a head and heart leader is knowing what balance of each of these leadership attributes is needed, and when.

There is no one-way model for leading with the head and the heart. The more attributes of a head and heart leader you can draw upon, in the right way and at the right time, the more effective you will be in the widest range of situations you might find yourself leading in.

Knowing what leadership attributes to use, and when, *is* the art of modern leadership.

It was in the wake of the 2019 Christchurch terrorist attack that Jacinda Ardern, one-time disc jockey and the former Prime Minister of New Zealand, first came to the world's attention as a head and heart leader. In the days following the attack, Ardern addressed the nation and managed to create a sense of belonging and embrace the pain the nation was feeling. She also signaled to the nation that inclusion and compassion in this moment were critical. This wasn't a moment that was all heart. Ardern also captured the anger of the nation and set the tone for how the country, and the world, should treat the gunman. "He may have sought notoriety," said Ardern. "But we in New Zealand will give him nothing—not even his name."

The day after the attack, Ardern visited the traumatized, grief-stricken Muslim community most deeply impacted by the violence. In a simple act of kindness and with deep insight into the context she was leading in, Ardern borrowed a scarf and wore it as a sign of respect to Muslim traditions. A simple act with profound consequences.

Ardern demonstrated the power of leading with both wisdom and perspective while at the same time demonstrating self-awareness, empathy, and humility. She was able to attend to the crisis both intellectually and emotionally.

Far from New Zealand, another modern leader captured the world's attention in 2022. The President of Ukraine, Volodymyr Zelensky, had a public life before politics that has become well known. Zelensky was a comedian and successful television producer who played a role as the nation's president before undertaking the role in real life. It is hard to know where the fictional world ends, and the real world begins.

It would be easy to critique Zelensky as an entertainer, staging his performance as a wartime president. But to do so would be a disservice to the head and heart leadership he has consistently displayed and the loyalty and combined sense of purpose he has built among Ukrainians in their darkest hour. Zelensky knows his role is to serve the people of Ukraine and he reinforces his role through the way he dresses, the way he communicates, and the way he demands action from the Western world.

Zelensky is masterful at "reading the room," adapting his message to the greatest effect for his audience. When speaking to politicians in the House of Commons in the UK, Zelensky channeled Shakespeare. When he spoke to the US Senate, he reminded them the United States is the leader of the free world. When he addressed the European Council summit, he invoked memories of World War II when

Hungarian Jews were murdered on the shores of the Danube.

While Ardern and Zelensky exemplify the style of modern leadership needed in the world today, remarkably this kind of leadership remains rare. The reason Ardern's and Zelensky's actions are notable is because we don't see modern leaders behave in these ways nearly often enough, especially not on the world stage. What makes Ardern and Zelensky stand apart is their ability to seamlessly integrate their personal qualities and authenticity with the authority invested in them through their formal roles.

It is clear the world needs modern leaders who understand they are continually learning and reshaping the best way they can lead in any given moment. Our world needs modern leaders who are eager to understand how they can have a positive impact on those around them.

We already have the skills and attributes we need to be modern leaders. The art of modern leadership is knowing which attributes you need, and when, as well as understanding that the modern leader we need in the world—is you.

Biography

Kirstin Ferguson AM is writer, columnist and company director. She is one of Australia's most prominent leadership experts. She is the author of *Head & Heart: The Art of Modern Leadership* and the co-author of *Women Kind: Unlocking the Power of Women Supporting Women* (Murdoch Books, 2018). Kirstin was named on Thinkers50 Radar List in 2021 and shortlisted for the Thinkers50 Distinguished Achievement Award in Leadership.

Note

1. Kirstin Ferguson, *Head & Heart: The Art of Modern Leadership* (London: Penguin Random House, 2023).

7

The Nine Derailers of Strategy

Ben Pring

New initiatives fail for a variety of reasons. One of the most common but underreported and under-analyzed is the inability of an organization to generate wide or deep enough alignment among different parties (business units, groups, vested interests et al.) around the product/service/strategy/idea.[1] Without such alignment, even the best new strategy will struggle to generate the momentum expected of it. Right now, with the business and technology landscape changing faster than ever, creating alignment has never been so important, yet never been more difficult.

Dealing with VUCA

Alignment is necessary throughout the lifecycle of a strategy but is of greatest importance in its early stages. Commonly, a new strategy is introduced in response to a change in market conditions: a competitor has introduced a new product, a client is no longer buying something, or a disruptive new vendor has emerged on the scene. This change produces significant VUCA (*v*olatility, *u*ncertainty, *c*omplexity, *a*mbiguity) and often an organization is forced to respond in the "stall zone," i.e., where old approaches are no longer working as well as they did, while new approaches have yet to take off.

Often the organization faces a "chicken and egg" scenario—forced to generate new revenues *from* the strategy to fund investments *in* the strategy. Typically, the new strategy is more complex and requires more sophisticated talent and behaviors than previously and takes place in a landscape that is dynamic and competitive. In the most complex situations, where industry-wide tectonic plates are shifting—as is the case at the moment in industry after industry—organizations face huge market change, which requires huge internal change, all the while keeping bookings going up *predictably* quarter by quarter.

Based on my experience, there are nine common derailers that leaders frequently encounter when trying to generate the necessary corporate alignment for their new strategies—along with nine solutions that can help. The nine derailers and their solutions fall into three distinct categories:

- **Strategic problems:** Where a strategic vision is inadequate, inappropriate, or unachievable.
- **Tactical problems:** Where a strategic vision is too theoretical, unmeasurable, or unactionable.
- **Intangible problems:** Where a strategic vision lacks a common cause or common foe, lacks consistency, and where the messenger is better than the message.

Strategic Problems

Derailer One: It's a Vision, but Not Visionary

In markets dominated by innovation, disruption, complexity, and impermanence, being able to articulate a strategic vision of a future state is extremely important. Without a sense of where a market, product, customer, or competition is going, a business (or business unit) is adrift amidst forces it doesn't fully understand or fully know how to command. A compelling strategic vision must be analytically correct, based on data and empirical evidence, but contain anecdotal "stories" that take abstract ideas and make them tangible. The vision must be inspirational and motivating and must resonate with both the most sophisticated in the "audience" and the novice. Most importantly, it must be "repeatable" by others, repeatability being the greatest test of listener/reader comprehension.

Too often unfortunately, leaders fail to create and convey strategic visions that meet these thresholds.

Solution One: Go Beyond the Comfort Zone

Demonstrating vision requires moving beyond the indisputably true— *the obvious*. It requires stating what is going to happen rather than what is happening. It requires placing a bet amidst great risk and uncertainty. If your vision requires none of these characteristics, it is not a vision, simply a recitation of current events. Stating your vision and asking others to believe it, to follow it, is asking a lot. Leaders shouldn't make this ask unless they recognize that in doing so, they are stretching their organization beyond the comfort zone. Doing this requires courage—if your vision doesn't require courage, think again.

Derailer Two: It's Visionary, But for Someone Else, Not Us

The other common failing of strategic visions is that while the vision may be an accurate reflection of what is going on in the market, be interesting and attractive, *and* be grounded in courage, it is in fact unrealistic and unachievable for the organization it has been created for.

These types of visions demonstrate an inadequate degree of analysis of the organization's current abilities, strengths, and weaknesses.

Solution Two: Develop Strategy for Your Organization, Not the Market at Large

Leaders need to stress test the strategic vision(s) they have, or are developing, against a variety of audiences, both internal and external. The key questions in these strength tests are: "Can we execute on this?" and "Does this make sense for us?" These questions should be posed so as to invite honest responses, rather than easy agreements, and the subsequent discussions should orientate around "why not?" reasons, i.e., "why shouldn't we do this?" In discussions and subsequent analysis, leaders should constantly be calibrating their refinement of the strategy against the litmus test of whether it will "work for this organization." Too often, strategic ideas, which, in their own right, are certainly valid, are not ones that the particular actual organization would be able to effect. Recognizing that good ideas are frequently not the right ideas is a key attribute of a successful leader.

Derailer Three: It's Visionary, and Doable, but a Long Haul

Another issue with strategic vision is that the promised land is visible but a long way off. To create a market-leading, profitable software portfolio for example, could take a professional services company at least 10 years. This is problematic simply because bosses, investors, and market commentators are, in our modern world, increasingly impatient, increasingly require instant gratification, and increasingly have alternatives beyond the one you are offering. Your vision may be visionary and may be right for the organization, but may also fail to last the distance; it could be supplanted by other more quickly executed visions which, though they might ultimately be less impactful, could satisfy other more immediate needs.

Solution Three: Identify Strategic Stepping Stones

Leaders should break the overall strategic vision into sub-phases with shorter time scales; for example, if generating a meaningful software portfolio (i.e., with market impact, material revenues with attractive margins, etc.) will take 10 years, this vision should consist of three phases, the first of two years, the second of three, and the third of five.

This "stepping stone" approach, when clearly delineated at the outset of the strategy pursuit, follows a "crawl, walk, run" approach, which articulates a perspective grounded in an appreciation of the realities of change. Leaders are sometimes reluctant to adopt this approach, given that the first stepping stone may seem underwhelming, whereas "wowing" their audience with the longer-term vision may generate more enthusiasm and buy-in. Calibrating the balance between dazzling your audience and laying out a carefully thought-through journey to the longer-term vision is an important part of developing and maintaining a broad and deep alignment.

Tactical Problems

Derailer Four: No Plan Survives Contact with the Enemy

This famous phrase, first attributed to nineteenth-century German Field Marshall, Helmuth von Moltke, is as true in 2023 as when first uttered, but its truth is widely ignored, unacknowledged, or unknown. Strategy teams (often utilizing external strategy consultants) devise sophisticated models and/or analytical maps of a market terrain, which are then handed down to operational teams to be executed, and which then come undone as these teams struggle to turn theory into reality. These teams run into von Moltke's aphorism, more colloquially articulated by boxer, Mike Tyson, as "everyone has a strategy until they're punched in the face." At this point the strategy as received is in effect DOA, and no amount of *pour encourager les autres* will rectify the situation.

This type of situation is what gives strategy a bad name. Airy, abstract, deliberately complex (but elegantly presented) ideas that are appealing in the artificial bubble of a conference room, but which wither on a Monday morning when a salesperson tries to put them into effect.

Solution Four: Have a Sailing Plan

Strategic plans do have value but need to be tempered against what can be best understood as a "sailing plan." The helmsperson of a sailboat may ultimately be heading to point A but knows that to get there may require first sailing toward point B, then C, then B again, before point A is reached. Due to wind and tide conditions, and other factors such as other boats and mooring peculiarities, the strategy of sailing (where are we going?) needs to work in tandem with the tactics of sailing (how do we get there?). Too often, strategists fail to understand or appreciate the role tactics play in executing a strategic plan; in fact, often tactical adjustments are perceived as a threat to the strategic plan.

Derailer Five: It's OK, But Not OKR

Derailer Five is perhaps the most important problem leaders face and is often the root cause of all the other eight problems. Put simply, the leader develops a strategy, which is discussed at length, debated, and dissected for hour after hour over, sometimes many months. Many different teams are exposed to the strategy under development and input and feedback are sought from many different parties up and down and across the organization. A consensus is reached; all the relevant players are on board; a celebratory bottle is opened, and the leader says, "OK, let's go." At this point, everyone involved drifts back to their desks and gets to work. Then, after a day, the various different parties start wondering and questioning exactly what it is that they're meant to be doing. What exactly is the goal? How exactly am I expected to do it? Who should I be working with?

Solution Five: Utilize Corporate OKRs (Plus Carrots and Sticks)

The answer to this problem is not new but is still not commonly deployed. The concept of Objectives and Key Results (OKRs) was developed at Intel in the 1970s and popularized by then CEO, Andy Grove. It later spread through other Silicon Valley startups (most notably Google) and has been widely credited with being instrumental to the success of many companies that followed in Intel and Google's wake. In *Measure What Matters*, John Doerr of leading venture capital firm, Kleiner Perkins (who was a salesman at Intel), outlined the key kernel of the OKR approach: "The key result has to be measurable . . . at the end you can look, and without any arguments . . . Did I do that, or did I not do it? Yes? No? Simple. No judgements in it."[2]

As with most "simple" solutions, actually making the solution simple is not simple. Getting all of the relevant parties (from board to

CEO to most junior employee) aligned to the strategy requires detailed OKRs up, down and across the organization. This is doable (otherwise Google et al. wouldn't be able to do it) but requires a lot of work.

Derailer Six: Strategies Are for Gods, Tactics for Mere Mortals

Having said that Derailer Five is the root cause of all of the other problems, Derailer Five has its own root cause, which is Derailer Six: namely, that leaders/strategists often enjoy the big-picture-thinking of crafting strategies, the intellectual cut and thrust of debating ideas and philosophies, and the "sexiness" of talking big numbers and grand ambitions, but have less interest—far less interest—in coming down to earth and doing the hard yards (outlined above in Derailer Five) of detailing how the strategy will be realized. That work is for the "little people"—the "operators" and "fixers"—the employees far lower down the organization.

Solution Six: Be Like Bradley

Omar Bradley, Chairman of the Joint Chiefs of Staff of the US military during the Korean War said, "Amateurs talk strategy; professionals talk logistics." GMs seeking to introduce and effect change should pin this statement above their desk. Instead of long, torturous discussions of this or that, or could or should, or perhaps or maybe or why not, leaders should force themselves and their staff to talk of getting things from point A to point B, of what material is to hand, what resources can be called on, what blockers are in the way, what terrain is to come. It might not be as fun as talking strategy, but talking logistics is far, far more important.

Intangible Problems

Derailer Seven: No Common Cause, No Common Foe

Cross-organizational alignment becomes harder the larger and more complex the organization becomes. Because this statement is obvious, its implications are often overlooked. Being a natural condition of the organization, less consideration is given than it should as to how organizational complexity hinders strategic execution.

Leaders striving to introduce new ideas into complex organizations need to have a deep understanding of the culture they are operating within; how entrepreneurial it is, how collaborative, how confident, how ambitious. Often, leaders new to the role fail to gage these characteristics accurately and implement strategies that are deeply ill-suited to the culture of the organization, though theoretically they appear at first glance relevant and appropriate.

Solution Seven: Create Campaigns for Common Causes and Common Foes

The idea of a military-style campaign against a competitor, enemy, or foe, can be hugely successful in generating the type of alignment needed to introduce a new product, service, or idea onto the market. By identifying a named competing organization and orientating internal communications toward and against this organization, the abstract can be made real—no longer are you trying to "launch a software product in the treasury management market," you are trying to beat "Organization X" in the treasury management market. Many leaders are reluctant to identify and name competitors and frame their objective as simply "growth." But by framing OKRs in more specific terms— "We will overtake Organization X in market share by 2024"—rather than simply stating "We will grow x% in 2024," leaders stand a greater chance of drawing to their cause the disparate teams and groups across the organization needed to achieve corporate goals.

Derailer Eight: Becoming Bored of the Vision (and Your Own Voice) Before Mission Is Accomplished

Any meaningful strategic vision that will deliver material and sustainable financial advantage will be calibrated in years, not months. Perhaps even decades. To that end, leaders responsible for the creation and execution of such a plan must be prepared to commit to it for the long run.

This means thinking about it constantly, talking about it constantly, nurturing it constantly, for the indefinite future. Some leaders are entirely comfortable with this; some, however, are not.

Often those attracted to ideas and existential discussions enjoy the "new" and the "next" but are less attracted to the "now," particularly a now that stretches out into an indefinite future.

Solution Eight: Deliver a Consistent Message, Consistently

Though this issue may seem somewhat comical and perhaps trivial, in people-based businesses—i.e., every business—consistency of messaging from senior executives is of paramount importance. Talking Head, David Byrne, was wrong in suggesting, "Say something once, why say it again?"[3] Leaders have to say the same thing again and again, and again, for far longer than they may be comfortable with.

Derailer Nine: The Messenger Is Better Than the Message

Paradoxically, a great messenger can sometimes prevent a message from being heard—the slides can be slick, the stage presence commanding, and the message makes sense in real time, but as the listener leaves the session, the audience have a nagging feeling of "what was the *there there there?*" In other words, where was the real substance? If you've experienced this as a listener, it's safe to assume that audiences have experienced this listening to you.

As a leader comes up through the ranks, the ability to present information becomes more and more important, and some leaders might end up feeling (perhaps consciously, perhaps subconsciously) that they can take *any* message and sell it. This is a very useful skill and has been the making of many a career. But where corporate-wide alignment around a new and challenging idea is required, the ability to sell something should not exceed the quality of what's being sold. If *only* the leader can deliver the message, the message is too complex and sophisticated for purpose.

Solution Nine: Upskill the Messengers, Simplify the Message

Leaders should develop the ability of a decently sized team to deliver alignment-focused messaging as well as (if not better than) the leader can. If this isn't the case, the leader's message will fail to travel as far, or with as much impact, as is necessary. To do this, leaders need to spend time with their teams, individually and collectively, transferring knowledge, insight, data, and specific talking points, to ensure their teams really "get it." This may seem an unnecessary burden to a time-starved leader, but it is a non-negotiable requirement, and there are no shortcuts. The medical training model of "watch one, do one, teach one" is a useful approach to use in this exercise—repeatability, as referenced above, being the key to understanding.

Lastly, if the team still struggles to relay the message, then the actual message should be revisited. A degradation of message quality as it travels down the ranks reflects on the message, not just on the messengers. Simplifying the message will be appropriate rather than just critiquing the messengers.

Summary Recommendations

Generating strategic alignment requires leaders to focus less on "where to go" and more on "how to get there." How do you do that?

- Engage regularly and frequently with peers and subordinate staff to sell, seduce, influence, and ensure buy-in and cooperation with the new strategy.
- Outline inspiring, relevant, material strategic visions that will endure beyond the next quarter or cycle.
- Implement strategic engagement mechanisms appropriate for the strategic context of the organization to build trust and partnership with other business units.
- Commit substantial personal capital in the pursuit of corporate goals; the hardest elements of generating alignment only come at a "human-to-human" level and require the investment of one's own humanity.

Biography

Ben Pring is a member of the Gartner for General Managers Program, Gartner's advisory services that consults with and counsels Gartner's most senior industry clients. Previously at Cognizant, where he was the co-founder of the Center for the Future of Work, he is the co-author of three best-selling books, including the award-winning *What to Do When Machines Do Everything*. In 2020, he was named to the Thinkers50 Radar list of up-and-coming thinkers whose ideas could make a positive difference in the world.

Notes

1. For reasons of brevity, products, services, strategy, ideas will be grouped together under the term "strategy" in the rest of this chapter.
2. J. Doerr, *Measure What Matters* (New York: Portfolio Penguin, 2018).
3. From David Byrne's song, "Psycho Killer."

8

Radical Empathy

How to Craft Effective Communications About Change

Tamsen Webster

A combination of huge uncertainty and the need to pivot and change direction at a moment's notice means that leadership in the current landscape is challenging. The success of your efforts in navigating these choppy waters—not to mention leading others through them—depends on how good you are at changing people's minds.

Except that people don't like to change their minds.

In fact, when challenged, people will often double down on their beliefs. They have to, really. Doing otherwise would force them to consider whether they're as smart, capable, and good as they think they are. Since that's a consideration basically all humans like to avoid, well, yeah, it makes your job tough.

So, what's a professional mind-changer like you to do? Well, first, remember that it's always about them, not (just) you. You're trying to create the change in them, sure, and that means you have a lot of work to do. But really, they have the much, much harder task.

Why? Because while you need to figure out the message that will move them (and yes, that's difficult in and of itself), they're the ones who actually have to move. And to create that movement, you pretty much HAVE to change what they believe . . .

Or do you?

For an example, let's look at how climate change conversations are difficult for both skeptics and environmentalists (see doubling down on beliefs, above). Studies have shown that when climate change skeptics were presented with other science they believed (such as germs and gravity), they moderated their position.[1] Similarly, in a different study, when environmentalists were taught to find multiple pathways in discussions (e.g., multiple ways to discuss climate change), those discussions were more successful.

Another concept, "paradoxical thinking" comes into play here. Basically, this is giving information to people that is consistent with what they currently believe but taking it to an illogical extreme. In one study, researchers used paradoxical thinking with people representing each side of the Israeli-Palestinian conflict. The results? People were more "conciliatory" in both thinking and behavior even a year later.

This helps explain why the climate change skeptics softened their position when presented with other forms of science they believe in: we need to give people information that validates their current thinking before we can change that thinking.

Why that works is because of another favorite concept of mine, "radical empathy." By stating the position of someone on the opposite side accurately and comprehensively, you can demonstrate to them that you have captured their view. Once you've validated the feelings that produced that person's thinking, they feel heard and understood. Human nature is such that, more often than not, they will reciprocate and will be more open to new information (especially if it's consistent with their thinking . . . see above!).

At the core of all of this is something I first said in a talk I gave at TEDxWilmingtonWomen a couple of years ago: "When two truths fight, only one lives." People cannot hold two truths in their minds at the same time and give both equal value. That's why the climate change skeptics softened their position. It's why people on both sides of the Israeli-Palestinian conflict softened theirs.

And there is one specific truth that, when brought into play, wins every time. You guessed it: the dominant truth, always, is people's belief that they are smart, capable, and good. That's what drives people's dominant *desire*: to be *seen* by others as smart, capable, and good.

That's why the environmentalists were more successful when they persisted in finding different pathways through difficult conversations. They had to find ways to talk about climate change that validated others' feelings, and the variety of reasons people felt as they did.

So, you see, to change someone's mind you don't have to change what they believe. That way often leads to tears, for all the reasons we just talked about.

No, instead, one of the most effective ways to change someone's mind is to present new information as a new *combination* of concepts your audience *already* believes or agrees with. Doing so validates their views, about both the world, and critically, what they want to believe about themselves.

When I work with clients to create these kinds of familiar-but-new messages, I use a structure I developed (my Red Thread® method) that is, at its heart, an exercise in this kind of radical empathy:

1. Articulate and validate what your audience says they want.

2. Articulate and validate something positive they get from their current approach.

3. Introduce a new approach in a way that's consistent with their previous thinking.

4. Validate that new approach with their beliefs about the world or themselves.

5. Let them come to their own conclusion . . . (yours).

6. Define and describe the actions that will make that change in thinking or behavior concrete.

7. Reaffirm how the new approach: (a) gets them what they want; (b) delivers the same benefit as their original approach; and, where applicable, (c) what additional benefits or outcomes the new approach brings.

Making the Case

Want to do this for yourself? Here's something to try . . . Fill in the following "script" for your idea or message:

> When I/we speak with: _____ [type of audience]
>
> They often want to know: _____ [common question your idea, product, or service answers]
>
> So they can: _____ [high-level goal to achieve]
>
> When looking for that answer, they often focus on: _____ [current perspective or approach]
>
> Rather than on: _____ [your/new perspective or approach]
>
> Yet I/we can agree it's true that: _____ [core value, belief, or discovery]
>
> That's why my/our answer is to: _____ [your recommended solution or approach]
>
> OPTIONAL: Which not only answers my audience's question, it also: _____ [additional key benefit it provides or need it fulfills]
>
> OPTIONAL: Here's how: _____ [actions or elements needed to fulfill your solution or approach]
>
> OPTIONAL: So would you be open to: _____ [first action you want your audience to take]

Filled in, it would read something like this:

> When I speak with leaders and message-makers of all sorts, they often want to know how they can make sure their ideas come across as powerfully as possible so that they can drive action from those ideas.
>
> When looking for that answer, they often focus on the significance of their ideas rather than on the structure of them. They focus on what makes the idea attractive and important rather than on what makes it strong. Yet I believe ideas are built, not found; research shows our brains build stories to make sense of

the world and the new information we encounter. In other words, every idea has a story because every idea IS a story . . . and only the strongest survive.

That's why my answer is to develop structured ways to reveal the story that built an idea in the first place. Doing that not only answers my audience's question (because it gives them a significant story to tell), it also gives them a way to make that idea strong enough to build on, and for you to get the change you desire.

Here's how you can do it yourself: start by filling out this framework, which includes all the essential story elements. Would you be open to giving it a try?

Don't miss what this script does. It gives you a more conversational way to start revealing the core message of the change you're trying to make, and of the story—the Red Thread—that built that idea in your mind in the first place. All the most important pieces of that story are built in, so see if you can spot in both the framework and the example the seven elements in the script I outlined previously.

Notice, too, that I framed the script in a fairly natural, conversational way. Ideally that means you'll be more likely to use audience-focused language in it, and thus keep it simple.

How or when could you use it? Anytime you need to craft important communications about change in your organization. If you're looking for a way to tackle communicating change to several different audiences, you can use it that way, too, and get a sense of which audience you want to start with, or of how your messages link together.

You could also use it as a first pass to help you reveal to yourself what your thinking about a desired change actually is. From there, you can identify which elements do and don't align with ones you need to find to make your story strong.

And, of course, once it's all filled out and strong, you can also use it as a great overview of your message—a quick conversational way to make the case for your idea or change.

Don't force people to double down. Lift them up on the strength of their own beliefs. Help them change into the person they want to be.

You may end up changing something far greater than a mind.

Biography

Tamsen Webster helps experts drive action from their ideas. The author of *Find Your Red Thread: Make Your Big Ideas Irresistible*, she honed her expertise through working with major companies and organizations such as Johnson & Johnson, Harvard Medical School, and Intel. In 2022, she was named to the Thinkers50 Radar list of up-and-coming thinkers whose ideas could make a positive difference in the world.

Notes

1. Climate Change Conversations Can Be Difficult for Both Skeptics, Environmentalists, August 10, 2019. https://www.apa.org/news/press/releases/2019/08/climate-change, Session 3169: "Leveraging Cognitive Consistency to Nudge Conservative Climate Change Beliefs," Saturday, Aug. 10, 4 p.m. CDT, Room 176c, Level One-West Building, McCormick Place Convention Center, 2301 S. King Drive, Chicago.

9

Leading Sustainability Transitions

Matt Gitsham

It's a tough time to be a business leader. Governments, and businesses, are grappling with the impacts of the war in Ukraine on the cost and security of energy and food supplies, wider inflationary pressures and impacts on the cost of living. And all this after only just beginning to catch breath and pick up the pieces after the Covid-19 pandemic.

In this context, it is becoming harder for leaders to retain focus on achieving Net Zero and dealing with the biodiversity crisis and wider environmental, social, and governance (ESG) issues around sustainability and human rights challenges. One recent study by KPMG found that 86% of CEOs feared a recession over the next 12 months, as a result of which half were planning on "pausing or reconsidering their existing or planned ESG efforts in the next six months," and 34% had already done so.[1]

Keeping ESG issues high on the agenda may have become more difficult, but the imperative to do so remains as pressing as ever. We continue to witness more and more temperature records being broken, and experience the effects of extreme heat, wildfires, crop failures, storms, and flooding across the globe. The authors of the February

2022 Intergovernmental Panel on Climate Change (IPCC) report concluded:

> The cumulative scientific evidence is unequivocal: Climate change is a threat to human well-being and planetary health. Any further delay in concerted anticipatory global action on adaptation and mitigation will miss a brief and rapidly closing window of opportunity to secure a liveable and sustainable future for all.[2]

The climate threat is urgent and existential.

It's not just climate we have to be concerned about. The October 2022 *Living Planet Report* shows that animal populations have experienced an average decline of nearly 70% since 1970. We've all grown up hearing about endangered species and certain animals being on the brink of extinction, but the scale of this problem has reached such epic proportions that scientists now speak of how we are living through the sixth mass extinction (a period of geological time in which a high percentage of biodiversity or distinct species die out. The fourth and fifth mass extinctions, for example, saw the death of the dinosaurs.) This mass ecosystem collapse is being driven by the clearing of wild spaces for agriculture, habitat loss due to climate change, pollution (from industrial chemicals, plastics, etc.), and hunting, and is as significant a threat to our way of life as the climate crisis.[3]

We face multiple human rights tragedies too. One area of human rights concern is that the number of people trapped in modern slavery has increased significantly in the last five years. Ten million more people were in modern slavery in 2021 compared to 2016 global estimates. According to the most recent study by the International Labour Organization and Walk Free Foundation, in total, 50 million people were living in modern slavery in 2021—and of these, 28 million were in forced labor and 22 million were trapped in forced marriage.[4]

One modern slavery flashpoint for business leaders is the concern about an unfolding genocide in Xinjiang, Western China, and forced labor in the cotton supply chain. Another area of human rights concern, as the #MeToo and #BlackLivesMatter protests continue to reverberate, is the ongoing systematic discrimination against women and Black people and people of color around the world.

A Business Imperative

Business leaders need to retain a focus on these challenges—encapsulated in the 17 UN Sustainable Development Goals—because it is important for society as a whole, and because it is important for their organizations.

In many areas we are already in the midst of "sustainability transitions": "fundamental transformational processes through which established socio-technical systems shift to more sustainable modes of production and consumption."[5] This disruptive change is afoot in a wide range of sectors, including energy, agriculture and food, manufacturing, chemicals, road transport, shipping, aviation, water and sanitation, construction, waste, finance, health, and telecommunications.

Around the world, the cost of renewable technologies is tumbling. Over the past ten years, the cost of offshore wind energy has fallen 61%, the cost of solar has fallen 89%, and the cost of batteries 83%.[6] This is disrupting the energy sector, supplanting fossil fuel electricity generation. In transport, annual electric vehicle sales are up at a compound annual growth rate of 68% over the same ten-year period.[7] Electric vehicles are disrupting the conventional internal combustion engine automotive sector, and change is coming to trucks, shipping, and even aviation too.

In buildings, a transition from gas boilers to electric heat pumps is underway. Similar changes are occurring in the chemicals, cement, and steel sectors, while in food, we are also seeing patterns of disruption, with substantial growth in plant-based foods and protein alternatives, as consumers seek health and environmental benefits.[8]

For the sake of their businesses, leaders need to understand and navigate these disruptions, to help their businesses adapt—no one wants to be the next Kodak, who saw disruptive change coming but failed to adapt. For the sake of humankind, business leaders need to help accelerate these transitions, and help them make a difference before it's too late.

Leading Disruption

But how? How can business leaders anticipate the disruptions that are coming to their sector and their business? How can they lead these disruptions, for the good of their businesses and for the good of all of us?

On one level, this is about deploying a range of familiar, tried and tested strategic foresight tools and leadership skills. Deploying the strategic foresight tools to gather data, anticipate likely scenarios around how disruption could influence the sector and your business, making choices about how to respond, and involving people from across your business and ecosystem in the sense-making and decision-making. It's also about deploying the leadership skills to bring people with you. It's not enough to recognize the need to adapt and take a different path; people across an organization or ecosystem need to understand and move together. There are leadership skills to employ here around creating the space to enable learning, trust-building, and empowered action among stakeholders who share a common goal— what some have characterized as "systems leadership."[9]

But to move from just navigating disruptive sustainability transitions in the interests of their organizations, to leading their acceleration in the interests of all of us, business leaders are increasingly required to make a mindset shift. The compass business leaders need to use to guide decision-making while navigating these disruptive changes has shifted.

In the prior model, a business leader's job was to maximize financial return on investment to shareholders within the confines of the law. Bigger issues in society were someone else's job. That model worked in the context of national companies that could be effectively regulated by governments, so that if the law needed to change to deal with some societal issue that needed addressing, government would do that.

Since the advent of globalization in the 1990s, with businesses operating across multiple jurisdictions, that model has broken down. With today's complex global challenges, governments cannot be relied on to provide the appropriate regulatory frameworks to deal with complex challenges on their own. This has led to increased expectations from multiple stakeholders (end consumers, direct customers, investors, employees) for businesses to play a leadership role on global challenges alongside others.

Business leaders no longer have a simple fiduciary duty to maximize return on investment to shareholders but multi-fiduciary obligations to create value for several stakeholders simultaneously. The goal is not simply maximizing ROI but maximizing the contribution to the UN Sustainable Development Goals. The constraint is not simply to act within the confines of the law, but additionally within the confines of global norms derived from UN treaties (such as the Universal Declaration of Human Rights, the UN Guiding Principles on Business and Human Rights, the Paris Climate Agreement, the ILO Core Labour Standards, the UN Anti-Corruption Convention), whether enacted into law by individual countries or not.

A New Compass

This is a different set of principles to be using as a compass for how to respond to disruptive challenges and requires skills in advocacy for taking this kind of leadership approach in the face of opposition from those operating with the previous mindset.

For example:

- How to engage well with investors where some are coming from a new perspective demanding more ambition on ESG, while others are operating from the prior model and are prioritizing short-term ROI?
- How to defend prioritizing creating value for multiple stakeholders to more senior leaders who are operating from a more traditional mindset?
- How to partner well with unconventional stakeholders to lead change in industry ecosystems, how to engage in advocacy and coalition building to develop alignment and mobilize action among stakeholders across an industry system,[10] for example, among suppliers, customers, and competitors, and maybe also NGOs and trade unions?

- How to engage well with policy-makers to advocate for more ambitious regulatory interventions from governments to help accelerate sustainability transitions in different sectors (e.g., through introducing carbon taxes, etc.)?

There are hopeful signs that at least some senior executives have recognized the business, environmental, and societal imperatives for change and have started to shift their mindsets and practices. But there are still too many leaders stuck in past perspectives. Business schools, management educators, and executive coaches have a key role to play in helping leaders think more broadly about how to create a better future. But ultimately, the buck stops with leaders themselves. They need to realize that leading through sustainability transitions is about both seizing the commercial opportunities and doing the right thing.

Biography

Matthew Gitsham is Professor of Sustainable Development and Director of the Hult Business for Society Research Impact Lab at Hult International Business School. He speaks and consults on sustainability, including topics such as sustainable development and sustainable business. He has advised organizations including the UN Global Compact, Unilever, IBM, HSBC, and GSK. In 2021, he was named to the Thinkers50 Radar list of up-and-coming thinkers whose ideas could make a positive difference in the world.

Notes

1. KPMG, *KPMG 2022 CEO Outlook* (KPMG, 2022). https://home.kpmg/xx/en/home/insights/2022/08/kpmg-2022-ceo-outlook/esg-and-diversity-trends.html.
2. IPCC, "Summary for Policymakers." In: *Climate Change 2022: Impacts, Adaptation and Vulnerability. Contribution of Working Group II to the Sixth Assessment Report of the Intergovernmental Panel on Climate Change* (eds. H.-O. Pörtner, D.C. Roberts, M. Tignor, E.S. Poloczanska, K. Mintenbeck, A. Alegría, M. Craig, S. Langsdorf, S. Löschke, V. Möller, A. Okem, B. Rama)

(Cambridge: Cambridge University Press, 2022), pp. 3–33, doi:10.1017/9781009325844.001. P. 33 https://www.ipcc.ch/report/ar6/wg2/downloads/report/IPCC_AR6_WGII_SummaryForPolicymakers.pdf.

3. WWF, *Living Planet Report 2022: Building a Nature-Positive Society* (eds. R.E.A. Almond, M. Grooten, D. Juffe Bignoli, and T. Petersen) (Gland, Switzerland: WWF, 2022). https://wwflpr.awsassets.panda.org/downloads/lpr_2022_full_report_1.pdf.

4. International Labour Organization (ILO), Walk Free, and International Organization for Migration (IOM), "Global Estimates of Modern Slavery: Forced Labour and Forced Marriage" (Geneva: ILO, 2022). https://www.ilo.org/wcmsp5/groups/public/—ed_norm/—ipec/documents/publication/wcms_854733.pdf.

5. M.A. Delmas, T.P. Lyon, and J.W. Maxwell, "Understanding the Role of the Corporation in Sustainability Transitions," *Organization & Environment*, 32(2) (2019): 87–97. https://doi.org/10.1177/1086026619848255.

6. K. Bond, and S. Butler-Sloss, "The Energy Transition Narrative" (RMI, 2022). https://rmi.org/insight/the-energy-transition-narrative/.

7. Ibid.

8. Meticulous Market Research, Europe Plant-Based Food Market by Type [Dairy Alternatives, Plant-based Meat, Meals, Confectionery, Beverages, Egg Substitutes, Seafood), Source (Soy, Wheat, Pea, Rice), Distribution Channel (B2B, B2C (Convenience Store, Online Retail)]: Forecast to 2029 (Meticulous Market Research Pvt. Ltd., 2022).

9. L. Dreier, D. Nabarro, and J. Nelson, "Systems Leadership for Sustainable Development: Strategies for Achieving Systemic Change" (Harvard Kennedy School, 2019). https://www.hks.harvard.edu/sites/default/files/centers/mrcbg/files/Systems%20Leadership.pdf

10. Ibid.

10

Navigating Paradoxes*

Wendy K. Smith and Marianne W. Lewis

What keeps leaders up at night? This question animated research by Oxford Saïd Business School professors Michael Smets, Tim Morris, and others in partnership with executive talent firm Heidrick & Struggles. To understand the challenges of contemporary leaders, they interviewed 150 CEOs from around the world. Their key finding? Paradoxes.

The CEOs struggled with ongoing tugs-of-war between irresolvable competing demands such as those between adapting to ongoing change and staying focused on the organization's core mission; leveraging global trends and scale while serving and competing in their local marketplaces; and achieving profits while addressing broader environmental and social concerns. Each issue the researchers identified had, at its core, a paradox. They state:

> Faced with competing, yet equally valid, stakeholder demands, CEOs increasingly face paradoxical situations of choosing

---

*This chapter was adapted from Wendy K. Smith and Marianne W. Lewis, *Both/And Thinking: Embracing Creative Tensions to Solve Your Toughest Problems* (Boston: Harvard Business Review Press, 2022).

between 'right . . . and right.' To get the 'best of both worlds,' CEOs need to first balance their personal paradoxes so they can find balance for their companies.

At their core, paradoxes juxtapose tensions, inviting leaders to move forward while dancing between opposing poles. They demand a move from traditional, binary thinking toward a more holistic, dynamic approach.

Expecting leaders to embrace paradox and thrive in uncertainty raises a pressing question: How? It's one thing to label experiences as paradoxical and another to respond effectively. We have spent the last 25 years studying how leaders navigate paradox. We've explored approaches used in corporate behemoths such as IBM and LEGO, startups and social enterprises, as well as nonprofits and government agencies. Here, we define paradox and related concepts of tensions and dilemmas, identify how paradoxes underlie leadership challenges, and introduce tools for their management within what we call The Paradox System.

Leadership Challenges as Paradoxes

Messy problems challenge leaders because they provoke dilemmas. Do I focus on short-term targets or plan for the long term? Do I ensure bottom-line profits or address social concerns? Do I do what's best for my company overall or what's best for individual employees? We feel tension—the experience of opposition. Dilemmas spark an inner tug-of-war that begs for a response.

Lots of scholars offer important suggestions about how to make clear choices when facing dilemmas. But before making a choice, we must look deeper to understand the nature of the problem. We need to unpack tensions, dilemmas and, most vitally, paradoxes (see Figure 10.1).

- **Tensions** include all types of situations where alternative demands are in opposition, describing presenting dilemmas and underlying paradoxes. Neither good nor bad, tensions can drive creativity and sustainability or lead to defensiveness and destruction.

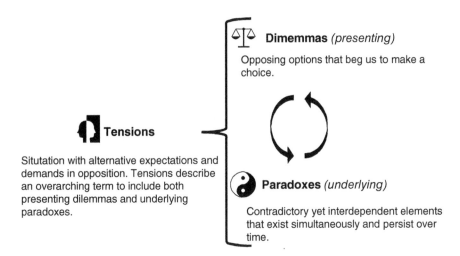

Figure 10.1 The language of tensions.

- **Dilemmas** offer opposing alternatives, each a logical solution on its own. Weighing up their advantages and disadvantages, we feel stuck. The pros of one option define the cons of the other, and vice versa. We chase our tails looking for the right and lasting solution. Moreover, when we decide between options, we can, over time, become stuck in a rut that leads to a vicious cycle.

- **Paradoxes** are interdependent, persistent contradictions that lurk within, presenting dilemmas. Exploring the options at a deeper level, we find opposing forces interlocked in a circular ebb and flow. Paradoxes may seem absurd as they integrate contradictions. Yet a more thorough investigation can unveil a logic to the holistic synergies of competing demands. Other researchers use words like polarity or dialectics in similar ways. We adopt the word *paradox* to align with a rich research tradition, and to reflect their often complex and mysterious ways.

In one of our studies, we explored how IBM leaders addressed innovation tensions as they shifted into cloud computing in the early 2000s. Business unit general managers all committed to ensuring ongoing success with their existing products while experimenting with new products for the future. Doing so sparked tugs-of-war over how to allocate their engineers' time, how to reward their salesforce, and how to structure the executive team. Leaders felt pressure to make choices. Yet underlying these dilemmas are paradoxes between today and tomorrow, core and explore, stability and change. These paradoxes are contradictory as options pull leaders in opposite directions, but also are interdependent in that they are interwoven and reinforcing. Moreover, the tensions never go away; they persist. No matter how many times you face conflicting forces between self and other, past and future, stability and change, while details of the presenting dilemma may change, the underlying paradox remains.

Why Now?

Paradox is not a new concept. These ideas emerged at the dawn of intellectual thought more than twenty-five hundred years ago. We draw from Eastern philosophy, such as that of Lao Tzu in the *Tao Te Ching*, from Western insights, including Greek philosopher Heraclitus, and from Southern philosophy with inspiration from Ubuntu and others. Intriguingly, these ancient insights emerged around the same time frame, but in different parts of the globe with limited communication. Over time, however, our societies have lost touch with the paradoxes that underlie our challenges as we have become more focused on linear, rational thinking.

Personal and global challenges call for paradox insights so that we can apply both/and thinking. In our research, we identified three conditions that accentuate paradoxes—*change*, *scarcity*, and *plurality*. Given accelerating technological change, waning natural resources, and expansive globalization, our world feels like the perfect paradox storm.

As challenges intensify, people are increasingly using paradox language, calling out interwoven opposites in these situations. For example, we have seen world leaders—from opposing political sides—call for both/and thinking. In an interview with author Brené Brown, former president Barack Obama stressed:

> It is both possible and necessary to see the paradoxes, the ambiguities, the gray areas, the absurdities sometimes, of life, but not be paralyzed by them . . . [M]y job is to look out for the safety of

American citizens as the American President. On the other hand, there is a universal interest in peace and fairness and justice outside our borders, and how do I reconcile those things, but then still be able to act as Commander in Chief and still be able to make a decision?

Senator John McCain, President Obama's own campaign opponent, shared a similar sentiment. In 2018, when McCain knew he was dying of a brain tumor, he called upon us all to seek options that connect rather than divide. "We weaken [our greatness] when we hide behind walls, rather than tear them down, when we doubt the power of our ideals, rather than trust them to be the great force for change they have always been."

Organizational leaders are also using both/and language to communicate their missions. Barclays unveiled a campaign it called AND—stressing that the 300-plus-year-old bank would only survive the next century by being relevant to shareholders and stakeholders and by making sure that it focused on markets and mission. The CEO of Starbucks responded to a question about whether the company was trying to offer customers a convenient, quick cup of coffee or build a space for gathering community. He explained, "But we don't believe there needs to be this type of a tradeoff . . . [O]ur third place can and will continue to unite both experiences." Yale University's marketing campaign also adopted such language: "Yale University is best defined by the word AND," explained one brochure. The university described an approach to education that is both big and small, inside and outside the classroom, advancing diversity and community. Political staffer Huma Abedin titled her memoir about living across disparate worlds *Both/And*. Look around.[1] Examples abound.

From Either/Or to Both/And Thinking

Effectively addressing tensions starts by noticing the paradoxes that lurk beneath our presenting dilemmas. Navigating paradoxes requires understanding tensions as double-edged swords—they can drag us down a negative path or catapult us toward a more positive one. In the same way that waves transmit energy that can be productive or destructive, so tensions can be unleashed for destruction and detriment or harnessed for creativity and opportunity.

Surfacing uncertainty, tensions foster anxiety. A dilemma presents contrasting options. Each valid on their own, yet with opposing pros and cons. Facing such uncertainty, we seek stable ground. We zoom in on the question and narrow our approach, applying more binary either/or thinking, evaluating alternatives, and choosing between them. Making a clear choice removes the uncertainty and therefore can minimize anxiety in the short term, but it also limits creativity and diminishes more sustainable possibilities. For example, leaders often adopt either/or thinking in response to their strategic dilemmas—move into a global market or stay domestic? Work virtually or maintain hybrid options? Develop digital solutions or nurture a human touch? These dilemmas can feel mutually exclusive, picking one option means rejecting the other.

At times, either/or thinking is useful. We may seek a clear choice when the consequences of the decision are minimal. We don't necessarily need to dig deeper into paradoxes to decide what food to order for the organization's picnic. Yet most of the time, either/or thinking can result in responses to dilemmas that are limited at best and detrimental at worst. Tensions spark defensiveness that leads us to want to make a decision. But making a choice can add to our problems. Psychology studies find again and again how we prefer stability and consistency over uncertainty and change.

Once we make a choice, we want consistency. We then become engrained in how we do something, becoming stuck in a rut. We stay where we are until something drastic forces us to change. This tendency leads us to overcorrect, swinging the pendulum to the opposite alternative and triggering an ongoing vicious cycle. Organizations often face swings between too much and not enough innovation, or too much and not enough focus on employee benefits. Ultimately, either/or thinking can trigger a vicious cycle that swings between alternatives—a long and winding road, with lots of chaos along the way.

What if we think differently? What if, instead of trying to choose between mutually exclusive options, we start by surfacing paradoxes that lurk beneath our dilemmas? Instead of choosing between alternative poles of a paradox, what if we ask a different question: how might we engage both poles simultaneously? How might we accommodate competing demands over time? Doing so invites us into both/and thinking, embracing tensions to enable more creative, effective, and lasting solutions. In doing so, we start to see the holistic integration that moves us beyond the binaries. Both/and thinking can open dialogue and fuel virtuous cycles.

The Paradox System

Through our research we find that navigating paradoxes involves using tools, which we integrate within The Paradox System. These sets of tools enable both/and thinking. As a memory aid, think ABCD: tools that shift how we think (*assumptions*) and build static structures (*boundaries*), while also shifting how we feel (*comfort*), and enabling adaptive practices (*dynamics*) (Figure 10.2).

Both/and thinking requires *assumptions* that help us cognitively hold opposing forces at the same time. The first step in shifting our approach is changing how we frame problems. Mindsets matter. Rather

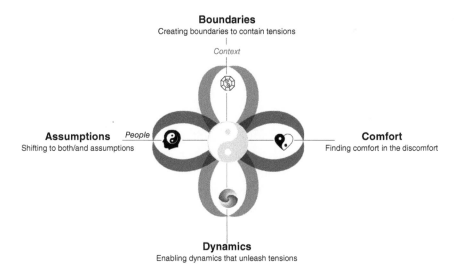

Figure 10.2 The paradox system.

than assume that the world is consistent, linear, and static, both/and thinkers assume that the world is contradictory, circular, and dynamic. We developed the Paradox Mindset Inventory (see https://paradox. lerner.udel.edu/), testing thousands of individuals worldwide. We find that those with a paradox mindset, who experience tensions and adopt both/and thinking, are more creative, effective, and satisfied in their jobs.

Boundaries involve structures that we build around us to support our mindsets, emotions, and behaviors as we confront paradoxes. Competing demands can lead us into a rut if we pick a side and then stubbornly defend it until we get stuck in a vicious cycle. Boundaries keep us from falling into such ruts. A higher purpose—an overarching vision that motivates and unites—reminds us why and how we engage with paradoxes. Creating structures that both separate competing demands, pulling them apart to value each, and connect them, finding synergies and integration, enables more sustainable solutions. Boundaries act as guardrails, keeping us from focusing too much on one side to the detriment of the other.

Comfort addresses our emotions. Tensions spark anxiety and defensiveness, which can trap us in either/or thinking. Yet the unleashing of creative options to address tough problems can be exciting and energizing. Navigating paradoxes requires leadership practices to surface and honor our initial emotional discomfort and find ways to be comfortable with the discomfort.

Finally, *dynamism* involves actions that foster continuous learning, encouraging shifts between competing demands. Paradoxes involve dualism and dynamism—two opposing forces constantly shifting one another. Dynamic actions allow us to capture the constant that is change, keeping us from getting stuck in an either/or rut, including leadership practices to encourage experimentation, seek serendipity and invite employees to learn to relearn.

Two interwoven insights emerged as we studied leaders applying these tools. First, the most effective both/and thinkers engage with all of these tools, enabling them to work together. Second, navigating paradoxes is paradoxical. Tensions are embedded in the paradox system. As shown in Figure 10.2, across the horizontal (people) axis are tools to engage the heart and mind. Often in conflict, heart and mind also reinforce one another. The vertical (context) axis represents tools that help frame a particular situation, fostering stable boundaries and enabling changing dynamics. Again, stability and change pull in opposite directions and foster synergies. Together, these tools support both/and thinking that addresses paradoxes both personally (assumptions and comfort) and contextually (boundaries and dynamism).

Leadership in an age of uncertainty requires navigating paradoxes. Learning to engage these interdependent contradictions enables more creativity and sustainability—and ultimately offers valued tools to address our greatest challenges.

Biographies

Wendy K. Smith is the Dana J. Johnson Professor of Management and Faculty Director of the Women's Leadership Initiative at the Lerner College of Business and Economics, University of Delaware. She earned her PhD in organizational behavior at Harvard Business School, where she began her intensive research on paradoxes—how leaders and senior teams effectively respond to contradictory yet interdependent demands.

Marianne W. Lewis is Dean and Professor of Management at the Lindner College of Business, University of Cincinnati. She previously served as Dean of Cass Business School, University of London, and as a Fulbright Scholar. A thought leader in organizational paradoxes, her work explores tensions and competing demands surrounding leadership and innovation.

Wendy Smith and Marianne Lewis are the authors of *Both/And Thinking: Embracing Creative Tensions to Solve Your Toughest Problems* (www.bothandthinking.net).

Note

1. Huma Abedin, *Both/And: A Life in Many Worlds* (New York: Simon & Schuster, 2021).

11

The WHY, WHAT, and HOW of Leadership

Paul R. Carlile

My last conversation with Clay Christensen was in his home in late October of 2019. I asked him about his health, and we talked about our families. Then he asked me what was new at work. I told him about the project I was leading to create a $24,000 low-priced online MBA and spelled out our innovative approach. Each course (module) would be focused on business problems as they exist in the world and not as they do in academic departments. The curriculum would be created and taught by interdisciplinary teams of faculty. And our target audience would be business practitioners supported by technology to enhance both synchronous and asynchronous peer-to-peer engagement.

Clay, whose 2008 book, *Disrupting Class*[1] had thrown out a challenge to traditional education models, turned to me and said: "Finally, an incumbent, a top university like yours, is disrupting itself."

The three years since that day have been very challenging as COVID hit just a few months later and creating this path-breaking approach had to be done all virtually and under increasing financial and human capital constraints. But it has been very rewarding as we graduated our first class of over 300 students in the summer of 2022 and we currently have nearly 1800 active learners with over 300 students more who graduated in December 2022.

Given the challenges and the successes, I have learned three leadership lessons. First, we had to articulate a strong vision of where we wanted to go and how it was different from other online programs. This established a mission-driven journey—that I call the WHY of leadership.

Second, we had to define and then create what we meant by business problem-focused module, by integrative assignments and capstone projects, new roles and how they were different from existing roles in the University. This established the things along the journey— that I call the WHAT of leadership.

Third, we had to establish the processes that would connect all the existing things (mostly learning outcomes) and roles with the new ones we were creating. This creates interdependencies to diagnose and then make thoughtful tradeoffs with the existing processes of the current University. Establishing these processes sustains the journey—it is what I call the HOW of leadership.

So, what do the WHY, WHAT, and HOW look like? Here are some examples, which illustrate the journey.

First, the WHY. We decided that we were not just going to be disruptive, but also distinctive to attract the right adult learner segment in the market and the right talent to help us create a program for them. This vision, pictured as a low price, yet high quality program at scale, allowed us to claim a new category in the market that our mission could be oriented toward. Business professionals who missed the opportunity to get an MBA in their twenties, thirties, or forties could stay in their current jobs and afford an MBA.

These adult learners were attracted to us because the curriculum and the faculty met them around contemporary business problems. Business practitioners would come to us because they could work closely with large numbers of their peers working on projects, sharing problems and the co-creating solutions for those problems. This WHY of the value we wanted to create also provided a vision and mission to attract and hire learning designers who were driven by it. It inspired faculty to join and sent a signal to skills sets of people outside of the education industry to fill new roles because they wanted to change the business education industry. We knew this was working because every single person we eventually hired could articulate how their WHY fitted into the WHY we were creating.

Second, the WHAT. Given the innovative vision, there were many new "things" that had to be defined, agreed to, chosen, or hired for. These were everything from defining cross-disciplinary learning objectives for a given week among faculty to agreeing to the integrative purpose of an end-of-module capstone project. From choosing the audio and video equipment for the Live studio, to hiring candidates for the "new" learning facilitator roles. All these new creations required significant attention from myself and others on the leadership team. Further still, though, these new things often stood in contrast and potentially in conflict to existing "things" in the larger University that we were dependent on for resources—current definitions, agreements, choices, and roles.

The learning facilitator role, for example, was new to the University and there was no precedent for it. So, as we created it, the University wanted to put it into a "known thing" bucket: it sounds like a TA (teaching assistant) or is it just an adjunct role? We spent significant time explaining how this role would help us scale the impact of the faculty (learning facilitators grade assignments and guide the students when they experience a problem in their learning journey), given that each course has over 400 students in them. They wouldn't be hired as faculty but would be a part of the teaching team and so we needed to professionalize the role with full-time benefits when positions seen as "similar" were part-time and temporary. As we created new things, this generated dependencies between those new things and existing things. This generated the next leadership challenge, which proved even harder to address.

Third, the HOW. Not surprisingly, when you have two things you need a process to meaningfully connect them, a HOW to define and then manage their dependency. So, much like in a network, nodes are things, and the links are the processes of HOW they are connected so critical information and resources can flow across them to complete a given task.

When creating new things, HOW they interface with other new and existing things is what brings the WHY to life. Most often problems between new things or new and existing things show up in the form of a personal conflict. People tend to blame the new person (role) or thing (new learning outcomes) rather than step back and diagnose whether there is a bad or missing process.

It takes strong leadership to get at the HOW of the conflict to diagnose and change and create to improve the HOW being used or address how it is breaking down. For example, the learning facilitator role was new, so therefore new to the learning designers and the faculty. Historically learning designers work directly with faculty, but this historical dependency between them stems from a traditional classroom size of 40 students and a curriculum that works in that setting. Since we use the learning facilitators to scale the presence of the teaching team and for grading our adult learners, it became critical for them to collaborate with the faculty and learning designers in creating assessments—because they know firsthand the delivery of the content and its assessment.

Early on, we faced significant challenges and conflicts between faculty, learning designers, and learning facilitators in HOW they would work together to produce the content required. Again, people will often blame the WHAT since the HOW is less concrete and more complex to understand. Leadership must attend to identifying breakdowns in the HOW and in improving them. This is perhaps the most significant effort required to bring the WHY to life and it remains dynamic and ongoing.

This WHY, WHAT, and HOW of leadership reminds me of the first conversation I had with Clay in early 1997. He asked me then what I thought about his shift of emphasis from disruptive technology (his first popular *HBR* article in 1995)[2] to disruptive innovation that was the core idea in his 1997 book *The Innovator's Dilemma*.[3] I told him it was the right shift—because "innovation" asks more questions about how disruption happens in the world—not just that it is driven by technology. But then I added a bit more—that the means of disruption could be thought of as a disruptive organization or more accurately as a "disruptive way of organizing." Clay laughed when I told him that because I taught organizational behavior, so he knew that's how I would frame it.

What I see more clearly 25 years later is that the WHY, WHAT, and HOW of leadership is the way we create disruption in the world in a deliberate and persistent fashion. By persistent, I mean to say that the WHY, WHAT, and HOW is a dynamic outcome that needs to be adapted as time passes and learning occurs, but also refreshed dynamically with those you work with weekly and presented afresh with those you are encountering for the first time.

In this way, the WHY, WHAT, and HOW of leadership becomes an overarching or meta way of leading that needs to be distributed across your leadership team and the larger set of stakeholders that you interact with and are dependent on for resources and opportunities.

This meta process that helps build a larger capability for distributed leadership and adaptability in your organization is the fourth lesson that naturally builds from the first three. This culminating lesson helps establish a disruptive way of organizing that is not just dependent on the leader, but other people who make up the organization. The specific circumstances of a given WHY, WHAT, and HOW of leadership become the means of helping others recognize their role in the META process of the WHY, WHAT, and HOW that distributes this larger means of leadership and adaptability across an organization. It becomes a shared language to frame opportunities and challenges that people see; to diagnose breakdowns and propose a path forward with others; and to sustain that journey with others into the future in an adaptive way.

These four leadership lessons become even more important during times of constraint and uncertainty because the vision, things, and processes are even more important to be distinctive to attract your market and attract talent. And distributing these leadership lessons across people in the organization not only helps sustain its innovative trajectory but also a shared WHY, WHAT, and HOW for adaption along the journey.

Biography

Paul R. Carlile is Professor of Information Systems and Senior Associate Dean for Innovation at Boston University Questrom School of Business. In addition to his influential research, he has developed award-winning experiential learning programs, including one in digital transformation with 380,000 learners, and a disruptively priced online MBA focused on business problems. In 2022, he was named to the Thinkers50 Radar list of up-and-coming thinkers whose ideas and actions are making a positive difference in the world.

Notes

1. Clayton M. Christensen, Michael B. Horn, and Curtis W. Johnson, *Disrupting Class: How Disruptive Innovation Will Change the Way the World Learns* (New York: McGraw-Hill Education, 2008).
2. Joseph L. Bower and Clayton M. Christensen, "Disruptive Technologies: Catching the Wave." *Harvard Business Review* (1995).
3. Clayton M. Christensen, *The Innovator's Dilemma* (Boston: Harvard Business Review Press, 1997).

Organizational Culture

12

Developing a Curious Culture at Work

Diane Hamilton

Curiosity is a key factor in the success of leaders from all walks of life: it helps them relate to the people and circumstances around them and seek out novel points of views and solutions. Organizations that embed curiosity in their culture also do better in terms of innovation and resilience. But how do you foster curiosity at a personal and organizational level?

When I started to research and write about curiosity, I began to recognize that I needed to do more than write about what it means to be curious. If my goal was to get people to be more curious, I needed to learn what inhibited curiosity. That required years of research and learning much more than I had ever anticipated about the things that hold us back at work.

What Is Curiosity?

I am often asked to define what I mean by curiosity. I look at curiosity as getting out of status-quo behaviors. We know from the Kodaks of the world that we can't rest on our laurels and hope that what worked in the past will work in the future. We must look beyond our cubicles, silos, and sometimes our industries. That can be a challenge when people hang onto the high they felt from something that worked well in the past. That is why leaders must recognize the link curiosity has with almost everything they want to accomplish at work.

I like to think of developing curiosity, like baking a cake. If you want to bake a cake, you mix ingredients such as flour, eggs, and oil, put the mixture into a pan, and place it in the oven, hoping for a cake. But, of course, you only get cake if you turn on the oven. Now think about the workplace, and instead, think of your cake as productivity and financial success. Organizations mix the ingredients of innovation, engagement, collaboration, and more, but no one gets cake if they don't turn on the oven. The oven in this scenario is curiosity. It is the spark to make sure those ingredients turn into success. This connection might seem intuitive, but there is a surprising lack of research regarding the relationship between curiosity and financial outcomes. Some top minds, like Harvard's Amy Edmondson, have discussed the connection on my radio show. Amy gave a terrific TED talk describing how the Chilean miners were saved because of the value of curiosity and collaboration.[1] So, if we know that curiosity is critical, then we must try to understand what inhibits curiosity at work.

What Inhibits Curiosity?

When I first started studying curiosity, I posted a Google alert to let me know when research or news came out about it (minus the eponymous Mars Rover, of course), and I rarely got notifications. In the last few years, the focus on curiosity has changed dramatically. The Google alerts never stop coming now.

Some of them are for anecdotal evidence, and others for new research. When I give talks to different groups, I sometimes include a slide from a study from the Fortune 500 top female executives, who were asked what they believed made them successful. Nearly everyone used some form of the word curiosity, whether it was getting out of status-quo thinking, asking questions, or being inquisitive. Most actually used the word curiosity. We have heard it from everyone from Oprah to Warren Buffett.

To support my findings about the value of curiosity, I looked at the popular research in the field, including Carol Dweck's *Mindset*,[2] Dan Pink's *Drive*,[3] and Simon Sinek's *Start with Why*.[4] In addition, I was fortunate to have many great Harvard professors join me on my radio show to discuss the value of curiosity, including Francesca Gino. She wrote a terrific piece for the *Harvard Business Review* on the business case for curiosity.[5]

Once I had the foundation for the importance and value of curiosity, it became critical to quantify what happens to it. There were curiosity assessments that detailed curiosity levels. So, for example, you could find out from Todd Kashdan's instrument whether your level was high or low.[6] That is a great instrument to create a starting and ending point to see if curiosity changes. However, what if it is low initially? What instrument was there to explain why? That is where I began my research.

Using experience working with assessments from writing my doctoral dissertation on emotional intelligence, I created the first and only instrument that determined what inhibits curiosity. So, if you are curious, I can tell you what I found. Four things inhibit our curiosity, including our fear, assumptions (that voice in our head), technology (under- and over-utilization of it), and our environment (everyone with whom we have had any interactions). I use the acronym of FATE to help people remember those factors. Some factors were not that surprising, while I had not anticipated others.

I expected fear to be at the top of the list. And it was a significant factor; however, you might be surprised to learn that all four factors were similar in how much they impacted our curiosity. Fear came up quite often in my initial research. Prior to writing my book, *Cracking the Curiosity Code*,[7] I started by posting a LinkedIn post asking people what kept them from asking questions in a meeting.

Overwhelmingly, people gave fear-based responses. No one wants to look unprepared or, worse, stupid. We have all sat in a meeting wishing someone would ask our question. But, when no one asks, we assume we missed something we should have known. It's human nature. It's also tied to the culture of an organization. If question-asking is encouraged, people are far more likely to overcome that fear.

Our assumptions can feed those fears. That little voice in our heads can make us shut down because it might tell us things like, "If I ask that question, they might just make me do more work without paying me for it," or "I don't want to explore doing that thing because when I did it last time, it was not successful." I often speak to groups where I hold up a glass of water and ask how much the water weighs. People yell out amounts like six ounces or eight ounces. Then I explain that it doesn't matter. What matters is how long I hold it. If I hold it for a few moments, it is not a problem. If I hold it for a few hours, my arm gets tired. If I hold onto it all day, I become paralyzed. It is like that with our negative thoughts. The more we hold onto that voice in our head telling us we won't like something, or it is too hard, or an endless list of other negative thoughts, we end up paralyzed. It is time to put the water down.

One factor that I found surprising was technology. I had yet to consider how much we either rely on or avoid it. At work, there are multiple generations, and sometimes the age you think has the best background in tech only occasionally has the foundation. We need to dig deeper to learn everyone's abilities. For example, imagine you had the intellect of Albert Einstein, and I just gave you a calculator and did not tell you how the math behind it worked. You might be the most outstanding calculator operator, but you might never become the best mathematician. Understanding how to build the best technology and utilize it to its fullest requires understanding why and how it works. At the same time, once we have a calculator, we must learn what it can do to utilize it best.

One of the factors that might be frustrating for people who have had their curiosity inhibited is what I call "environment." Our environment is everything from our parents, teachers, co-workers, leaders, friends, social media, and basically, everyone with whom we have interacted in our lives. You might ask why it is essential to go back in time to understand those relationships if we can't change them. We cannot change what happened, but we can change how we feel about the impact now. Once we recognize we didn't go into the job or field that we loved because someone in our family told us that was not a good thing to do, or we stopped being interested in creating certain things because our teachers had so many students, they could not take time to foster our interests, we can revisit some of our choices and rewrite that script that affects our assumptions and our fears.

How to Fix It?

When I train organizations, they learn from the Curiosity Code Index which things inhibit them, and then we work on developing a sort of personal SWOT analysis that helps them create SMART goals. Since this is compressed into one chapter, you can begin doing some of this independently.

Write down the four letters of FATE, and next to each letter, write your personal answer:

- **F (Fear):** List some things that keep you from asking questions in a meeting.
- **A (Assumptions):** List some of the things you tell yourself that keep you from exploring new things.
- **T (Technology):** List some reasons you under- or over-utilize technology.
- **E (Environment):** List reasons you did not explore your curiosity based on your relationships.

Once you have your issues for each area, you can set goals to overcome them that are measurable and list potential outcomes to expect. Include who can support you in your endeavor and any potential threats you would need to overcome, in straightforward ways. When I train organizations, we spend about half the time dealing with employees' issues, and then the other half we spend on the organization's overall issues impacted by curiosity.

Usually, leadership has asked for help with innovation or engagement and multiple other leadership-based skills. Employees love the part of the training where they can give feedback on how the organization can learn to be more curious to help in these areas. It is not unlike how Disney went about improving turnover in its laundry division. They went to their employees and asked, "What can we do to improve your job?" They got significant and helpful suggestions like putting an air vent over my folding table or having my table be adjustable, so my back doesn't hurt.

Leaders can go to their people and ask for input. Leaders can emulate the curious nature they want to see in their people. When employees see leadership asking questions and not shutting them down for providing suggestions, it can create a massive culture shift. Once you light that spark of curiosity, everyone can get cake.

Biography

Diane Hamilton is the CEO of Tonerra, a radio host, keynote speaker, and former MBA Program Chair at the Forbes School of Business. She is the author of *Cracking the Curiosity Code* and creator of the Curiosity Code Index®, the first assessment that determines inhibitors of curiosity. In 2020, she was named to the Thinkers50 Radar list of up-and-coming thinkers whose ideas can make a positive difference in the world.

Notes

1. Amy Edmondson, TED Talk, https://www.youtube.com/watch?v=3boKz0 Exros.
2. Carol Dweck., *Mindset* (New York: Random House 2006).
3. Daniel H. Pink, *Drive* (New York: Canongate Books, 2011).
4. Simon Sinek, *Start with Why* (London: Portfolio Penguin, 2011).
5. Francesca Gino, "The Business Case for Curiosity," *Harvard Business Review*, September–October (2018).
6. Todd Kashdan, https://www.sciencedirect.com/science/article/abs/pii/S0092656609001275.
7. Diane Hamilton, *Cracking the Curiosity Code* (New York: Author, 2019).

13

Is Your Company Alive?

Mehran Gul

The science of complexity is changing our understanding of what organizations are and how they should be run.

An army ant is a simple being. Perhaps the simplest. It is nearly blind and minimally intelligent. If a hundred of them are placed on a flat surface, they will move aimlessly in circles until they die of exhaustion. But when half a million come together in a rainforest, they organize into a coherent army—an aggressive swarm that can devour all prey in its path, capable of destroying edible life over a dense forest the size of a football field in the course of a single day.

It's not all fire and fury. Ants exhibit their nurturing, altruistic side by building ant colonies which increase the survival probability of the community. An individual ant cannot regulate its body temperature; ant colonies can control their climate. An ant's memory is almost non-existent; ant colonies can retain memories longer than the entire lifespans of their members. Individual ants die off every year or so; ant colonies can thrive for decades.

It seems that, like many of us, ants lead dual lives. A solitary ant has a distinct physical individuality. But it can also aggregate with other ants to merge into something larger than itself. Edward Wilson,[1] a biologist at Harvard, thinks that ant colonies are superorganisms; living, breathing entities that possess collective intelligence and intention. A whole far greater than the sum of its parts. The collective sophistication of an ant colony stands in stark contrast to the individual simplicity of an ant.

Superorganisms like ant colonies are just one example of complex adaptive systems which occur widely in nature. Melanie Mitchell, a computer scientist who has worked at the Santa Fe Institute, describes these systems as self-organizing superstructures which emerge out of the interaction of relatively simple parts in the absence of a central authority.[2] The study of complexity is a burgeoning interdisciplinary field which is being used to investigate systems as diverse as brains, cities, and economies. Stephen Hawking predicted that complexity will be the science of the twenty-first century.

This approach to studying collective behavior is steadily gaining ground in our thinking about organizational behavior. In his book. *Scale: The Universal Laws of Growth, Innovation, Sustainability, and the Pace of Life in Organisms, Cities, Economies, and Companies*, Geoffrey West, a celebrated Stanford physicist, writes that there can be a predictive science of companies paralleling a science of other emergent complex systems which can help us understand how companies grow, mature, and die.[3]

What does this mean for how organizations are run in practice? Managers and management thinkers have long looked at organizations the way engineers look at machines. They reduce the whole to the behavior of its parts and enforce rigid hierarchies and rules to arrive at their desired objectives. This approach worked well through the industrial age and led to significant strides in production. But if we now understand organizations as living biological systems, then for them to prosper, this mechanistic approach needs to yield to something more organic in character.

Professor Julian Birkinshaw, of London Business School, believes that this means companies need to change the way they work and move from bureaucracy to emergence.[4] He cites the example of Oticon, a Danish hearing aid manufacturer, which in its efforts to stay relevant in changing market conditions and compete with well-resourced new entrants, ripped up its top-down structure and replaced it with the concept of the spaghetti organization.[5]

Founded in 1904, Oticon pioneered the manufacture of hearing aids and was the first hearing instruments company in the world. In the 1960s, it was the world's leading hearing aid manufacturer but in the 1970s its market share started to decline as larger, better-resourced, broad-based consumer technology firms like Siemens, Phillips, Sony, and 3M entered the market with a newer generation of hearing aids. By the 1980s, Oticon—the company that virtually invented the market for hearing aids—was left with only 7% of the market share and was rapidly losing money.

In 1988, Lars Kolind, a former management consultant and business school professor, was brought in as CEO to turn around the fortunes of the company. Kolind realized that he could not compete with his larger rivals on technology or resources—they were simply too big—so his competitive advantage had to be something else. In his view, that advantage would come from redesigning the organization itself; he would have to make Oticon a uniquely innovative, fast-moving, efficient, nimble organization that could not be easily imitated by its powerful but lumbering rivals. In short, he wanted to shift the focus from *technical* innovation to *management* innovation.

In 1991, Kolind brought about a radical redesign of Oticon's organizational structure. He abandoned formal hierarchical relationships, reorganized resources into self-organized project teams, and completely eradicated paper-based procedures, replacing them with electronic communications—still a novelty in the early 1990s. He called it, "a spaghetti organization of rich strands in a chaotic network." The idea for the organization came from his frustrations in his former jobs where he thought management exercised too much control but seldom made a positive contribution to the development of the business.

Kolind thought his main task was to figure out how to liberate individuals from corporate fetters and to create the right kind of environment where employees behaved as individuals rather than small cogs in a big machine. Instead of over-engineering plans and budgets from the top, he wanted to empower people to make products by self-organizing around projects and pursue opportunities that they thought would be beneficial for the company. In short, he had to deconstruct the organization and create a new organizational model in which permanent departments were replaced with continuously changing project teams. The company essentially had to be dis-organized.

The result of the deliberately engineered "total chaos"—as Kolind termed it—was that the company returned to profitability by the mid-1990s. When Kolind stepped down as CEO in 1998, he left the company in a strong competitive position. In April 2022, Demant—Oticon's parent company—sold Oticon to Australian company Cochlear Limited for DKK850 million (approx. $120 million). Oticon's profitability has deteriorated in recent years, but one measure of its long-term success is that it has weathered multiple crises and endured for more than a hundred years. Not many companies do that.

Geoffrey West, the Stanford physicist, points out that the mean life of a company is around ten years. Less than half of 1% of all companies live past a hundred. He compares companies to cities—a useful comparison as they are both forms of social organization. "Are cities and companies just very large organisms that grew out of biology?" He asks, "Is San Francisco an elephant? New York a great big whale? Is Microsoft a beehive?"[6]

We often use biological terms when we talk about business and management—the DNA of the company, the ecology of the marketplace, the ecosystem of an industry. Is this simply borrowed language or is there something more to these metaphors which hint at the underlying biological fabric of these social structures? he wonders.

West points out that cities and companies are both examples of different forms of organic communities that have grown on this planet. But while cities almost always endure, companies almost always do not. "It's extraordinarily difficult to kill a city," he says, "we've dropped atom bombs on cities and thirty years later they're still thriving." Not so for companies. "It's very easy to kill a company. Almost all of them die," he adds. "There are very, very few companies that are one to two hundred years old," and most of those are in specialized niches.

Why? West thinks that cities endure but companies do not because cities tolerate crazy people. "Innovation is associated with super-linear scaling, that's what cities do, they open-up as they grow, they get more diverse, they get more interesting." He says that companies are innovative when they are small as they are more about ideas than about structure and process but as they grow larger, they basically become its bureaucracy and administration and the innovative part gets squeezed out, leading them to ossify and die.

Leaders and managers concerned about their companies' longevity and effectiveness need to figure out ways to experiment more with their organization's form so it can better serve its function. Most companies pay limited attention to innovation and most of the ones that do often focus narrowly on technological or process innovation. Companies that stay relevant and endure in the future will have to develop a competence in managerial innovation and derive their competitive advantage in large part from figuring out radically new ways of working.

Our understanding of what organizations are and how they should be run is evolving. We may just find that the way we work now might eventually be seen as being not dissimilar to a group of ants wandering aimlessly in circles. What comes next will remake organizations so they can be places where people can unleash their creative fire and fury.

Biography

Mehran Gul is the author of *The New Geography of Innovation* (forthcoming), which charts the rise of new tech companies around the world, and won the Financial Times/McKinsey Bracken Bower Prize for writers under 35. In 2022, he was named to the Thinkers50 Radar list of up-and-coming thinkers whose ideas could make a positive difference in the world.

Notes

1. Cited in Steven Johnson, *Emergence: The Connected Lives of Ants, Brains, Cities, and Software* (London: Penguin, 2001).
2. Melanie Mitchell, *Complexity: A Guided Tour* (Oxford: Oxford University Press, 2011).

3. Geoffrey West, *Scale: The Universal Laws of Growth, Innovation, Sustainability, and the Pace of Life in Organisms, Cities, Economies, and Companies* (London: Penguin, 2017).

4. Julian Birkinshaw and Michael J. Mol, "How Management Innovation Happens," *MIT Sloan Management Review*, 47(4) (2006).

5. Julian Birkinshaw and Stuart Crainer, "Oticon and the Spaghetti Organization," *Business Strategy Review*, January (2007).

6. Geoffrey West, "Why Cities Keep on Growing, Corporations Always Die, and Life Gets Faster," talk given at The Long Now Foundation, July 2011.

14

Staying in the Know in Extraordinary Times

Maja Korica

Environmental disasters, war, disease, and other extreme events. Rapidly changing industries and careers. New technologies. Work intensification. More connections. Less certainty. We live in highly fluid times—times that demand constant attempts at order, or at resilience, lest we are lost in their increasingly precarious tides.

We feel this increasingly, perilously unsteady world individually: self-help books on personal resilience abound. We discuss and arbitrate it politically.

Implications for organizations matter too. Most notably, what does our present-day systemic precariousness—what I call *the fluid now*—mean in terms of the skills that executives (and their staff) need to develop, and corporations should support?

A decade ago, my colleague Professor Davide Nicolini and I observed seven chief executives running major healthcare organizations in the UK. Their lives involved constant juggling of multiple issues with immediate, mid- and long-term implications, complex lines of accountability, countless stakeholders (from patients and their loved ones to medical staff, local communities, ministers, and civil servants), and constantly shifting expectations. Amid that, we saw active efforts to keep up with the shifting tides around them, but also to "know the unknown"—remain attuned to major problems lurking just around the corner, before it was too late to do anything about them.[1]

Such practices eventually became habit, which also brought further challenges: how do you remain sensitive to a changing environment without becoming entrenched in certain ways of working and therefore certain boundaries of the world as you've made it known to you? As Anaïs Nin put it, "We don't see things as they are, we see them as we are."[2] To be attentive to a constantly changing world, we must keep changing too.

All of this was already highly relevant to executives running complex organizations before 2020. Then, Covid-19 hit.

The pandemic was a truly extraordinary event—"out of the common order," as per its Latin origins. Though providing care amid crisis was familiar, it nevertheless disrupted many of the certainties our chief executives relied on to keep abreast of their organizations, close physical proximity to colleagues and unplanned verbal communication most of all. In this, they were not alone. In a tale now acutely familiar to office workers around the world, buildings were closed to all but a few, customary connections were maintained through online meetings and travel stopped, and staff retreated behind Zoom screens.

Soon, organizations adapted, however. "You're on mute" became a ubiquitous part of working life and so inevitably an internet meme; long-standing workplace institutions like commuting (and offices more broadly), presenteeism and advancement through social reproduction became openly, widely questioned. The possibility of doing better—better work, better organizations, better management, better capitalism—took center stage.

At a time when knowing what was happening was perhaps most important, executives' comfortable familiarity regarding *how to stay informed* was similarly wholly upended. While the pandemic brought much attention to senior leaders' communication, leadership, inclusion, presence, and related issues, it brought less to, well, attention itself; to the critical challenge of adjusting to and navigating executive attention in line with both a disrupted world and the emerging structures we have developed to deal with it.

So, how can leaders work to pay (better) attention? That is, how can they (better) stay in the know amid changing times and constantly evolving organizations? My argument is that this is central to better leadership and better organizations.

The Work of Staying in the Know

When Davide Nicolini and I shadowed the healthcare chief executives, they told us that a central problem was not knowing about problems earlier. This concern was typically phrased as "How can I have not known about this until now?"—in other words, becoming aware of an issue too late. Implied in this was a truism that to manage an issue, you first need to know about it.

This challenge—how to stay ahead of emerging issues by being aware of matters before they escalate into problem territory—was addressed via constant and dedicated, albeit explicitly rarely acknowledged work. We called it "staying in the know," to contrast it explicitly with the more familiar "being in the know," which holds a certain stability. The latter does not recognize that such knowing does not just happen—it is explicitly worked on. It can also hold you back; just because you know what's going on now doesn't mean the same knowledge will serve you well next month, as circumstances shift.

What did staying in the know entail? It relied on what we called *personal knowledge infrastructures*: individual assemblages of *people*, *tools*, and *priorities*, through which executives' attention was filtered and the boundaries of their known world reinforced. Importantly, these were mostly residual from experience, reinforced by context (e.g., experience of their senior teams, personal preferences regarding meetings, externally imposed targets), and rarely explicitly reflected on. Most often, they became visible only when disaster hit, i.e., when an issue crept up on them which the infrastructure had mistakenly failed to highlight which ended up having considerable (negative) effects.

This was in part because the infrastructure's habitual nature set several traps, including being attuned to information and sources that had previously been useful, but not for issues increasingly in prominence now.

Avoiding such traps critically relied on purposeful mindfulness: recognizing the importance of staying in the know, inserting pauses to collectively reflect (e.g., with executive teams and/or coaches), and prioritizing this as a regular practice, in conversation with aids such as Figure 14.1. The alternative was being blindsided and rushing to correct—much harder to do against the time pressure of an impending crisis, than with the comfort of dedicated time beforehand.

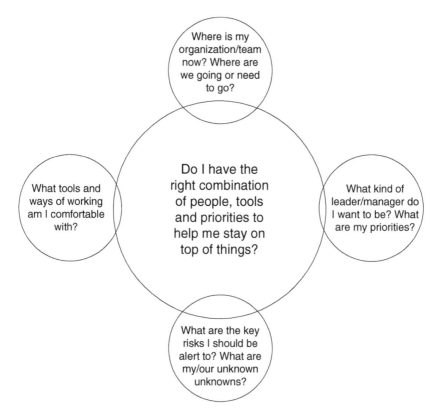

Figure 14.1 Visual aid for continued reflection on personal practices of staying in the know.

(*Source:* Adapted from Nicolini, Korica, and Ruddle, 2015).

Better Habits for Extraordinary Times

So, what can executives and leaders do to further adjust their information practices to extraordinary realities, such as the Covid-19 pandemic? Getting rid of habits wholesale is neither possible nor realistic. Instead, it is about building *better habits*, including those that purposefully destabilize emerging certainties and put in breaks, so that when faced with crisis you do not rush in, based on existing answers, but complexly explore to more complexly understand. This approach is based on three critical principles for staying in the know in extraordinary times: *connection*, *diversity*, and *serendipity*.

First, there is a tendency when facing crisis to retreat behind the walls of c-suites to strategize and respond, which often implies discussion with a narrow, pre-defined group of fellow executives. This removes leaders from the front lines and maims any subsequent decisions, which may well be based on limited understanding as a result. Instead, prioritizing **connection** means reaching out immediately and widely, to build a more complex picture of what is happening, why, and with what consequences.

This principle is necessarily supported by **diversity**: the possibility of building complex pictures is highly limited by the homogeneity of those consulted. Staying informed to stay ahead should therefore be reinforced by a principled and practiced commitment to seeking out diverse voices: across hierarchies, geographies, and lived experiences.

Here, executives might wish to ask themselves two questions: when did I last speak to someone new? And when did they last tell me something that took me aback or surprised me? If the answer to both is "far too long ago for comfort," corrective action is needed and fast.

Relatedly, and finally, purposefully reinserting **serendipity** is critical. Executive diaries and lives can quickly become hemmed in by the familiar people, places, tools, conversations, and priorities. These can only be disrupted if opportunities to seek out diverse connections are purposefully sought, by making room for the unfamiliar without an obvious aim in mind.

The principles are thus necessarily aided by *three key practices*:

- **Informal interactions over formal meetings:** One executive we observed relied heavily on a close group of experienced executives, a powerful network of industry insiders, an advanced information system giving live performance data, and highly structured accountability meetings to stay ahead of issues that might impact their organization. Importantly, though, such systems were reinforced by purposefully serendipitous informal interactions, which the CEO created by randomly visiting different hospital wards in the evenings and at weekends to hear directly from staff. This allowed them to identify a major staff issue, which their COO did not inform them of, and to get ahead of managing the widespread discord before it enflamed fully.

- **Technologies to connect over disseminate:** The pandemic brought with it a dramatic normalization of communication technologies like Zoom and Teams. But the opportunity they presented through flattened hierarchies and broader inclusion in meetings was too often lost, as executives scrambled to put them to work to disseminate key decisions and messages, rather than prompt more open conversations. Such technologies can be engaged differently, however, to facilitate greater serendipitous sharing, for instance, via executives introducing regular "check-in" sessions with randomly selected staff in groups of 5–10 across levels, divisions, and geographies. The role of the executives there is to reinforce the overall aim of learning and promote an environment of psychological safety at the start, asking open questions, such as: "What issue are you most worried about right now and why?", and listening attentively to the answer.

- **Pauses over speed:** For decades now, business leaders have been encouraged to face ever-increasing disruption by prioritizing speed above all (John Kotter's famous 1995 change management model,[3] whose first step is "establish a sense of urgency," is but one example). What this presumes, however, is that executives know where exactly they need to urgently go, i.e., what the problem is in the first place. Amid increasing instability, relying on existing certainties is a fool's errand. This can escalate into what colleagues have called "dysfunctional momentum"[4]—a misdiagnosis at the start, resulting in an inappropriate reaction that becomes the clung-to response, even as the environment throws up more warning signs that we may be off course. To disrupt this requires instituting purposeful pauses to enable serendipitous, diverse connections, and so increase chances of better diagnosis and continued correction en route.

Such practices inevitably require different leadership and leaders. As my colleagues Amy Edmondson, Kathleen Sutcliffe, and others have long stressed,[5] during heightened uncertainty, clinging to hierarchical relationships based on distrust, established certainties borne from experience, and ego reinforced by status is a recipe for disaster.

Instead, key *supporting conditions* for wiser, adaptive attunement to a changing world include *openness*, *humility*, and *trust*. Openness to other perspectives and answers, humility as to your own perspectives and answers being inherently limited, and trust that collective wisdom is necessary for better adaptation, but also that senior leaders will not punish staff for sharing "bad" news or insights that challenge preferred certainties.

Beyond Naïve Organizations

In 2009, a group of scholars[6] identified a phenomenon that they called *naïve organizations*. These organizations meet extreme situations by chance, yet find themselves little prepared, with their leaders unwilling to entertain these as likely, or even legitimate risks. Even before the Covid-19 pandemic, such obstinate clinging to the familiar was foolish, given our VUCA[7] world. In its aftermath, it is beyond naïve; it's reckless. Uncertainty is our new normal. Figuring out how to lead and manage differently is and will remain a pressing concern.

To know and therefore to be able to respond to a changing world, we must constantly adapt how we know it too—the work of staying in the know. Being informed, and relatedly attention, are therefore critical components of wiser management and leadership, not a by-product of their supposedly more important facets. It's time senior leaders paid more purposeful attention to it, lest their customary patterns lead them astray.

Biography

Maja Korica holds the senior academic position of Reader in Management and Organization at Warwick Business School, University of Warwick (UK). A qualitative researcher, she has closely observed boards and chief executives in the public sector over long periods of time to better understand their work and challenges. Her most recent funded study is on coordination on the ground during refugee emergencies. In 2017, she was named to the Thinkers50 Radar list of up-and-coming thinkers whose ideas could make a positive difference in the world.

Notes

1. See D. Nicolini, M. Korica, and K. Ruddle, "Staying in the Know," *MIT Sloan Management Review*, 56(4) (2015): 57, as well as D. Nicolini, and M. Korica, "Attentional Engagement as Practice: A Study of the Attentional Infrastructure of Healthcare Chief Executives," *Organization Science*, 32(5) (2021).
2. A. Nin, *Seduction of the Minotaur* (Athens, OH: Swallow Press, 1961).
3. J. Kotter, "Leading Change: Why Transformation Efforts Fail," *Harvard Business Review*, May–June (1995).
4. M.A. Barton, and K.M. Sutcliffe, "Learning When to Stop Momentum," *MIT Sloan Management Review*, 51 (2010): 69–76.
5. See, for instance, F. Rashid, A.C. Edmondson, and H.B. Leonard, "Leadership Lessons from the Chilean Mine Rescue," *Harvard Business Review*, 91(7–8): (2013): 113–119; K.E. Weick, and K.M. Sutcliffe, *Managing the Unexpected: Resilient Performance in an Age of Uncertainty* (Hoboken, NJ: Wiley, 2007).
6. S.T. Hannah, M. Uhl-Bien, B. Avolio, and F.L. Cavarretta, "A Framework for Examining Leadership in Extreme Contexts," *Leadership Quarterly*, 20 (2009): 897–919.
7. VUCA = volatile, uncertain, complex, and ambiguous.

15

Stop Quiet Quitting Your Life

Ori Brafman and Rom Brafman

Back in 1907, well before the term *quiet quitting* (disengaging and dragging your feet at work) invaded the lexicon and the collective consciousness, the father of American psychology, William James, sounded an alarm. Don't worry, this isn't a history lesson, but it's worth our time to unpack what James had to say.

"Compared with what we ought to be," James warned in one of his final writings, "we are only half awake. Our fires are damped, our drafts are checked."[1] Unfortunately, the poetic language may have obscured his message. Nobody fully grasped the gravity of what he was saying.

To give it some modern context, if you sat with James in a bar today, he might swivel his stool, turn to you, and say something like: "Dude, you're in a fog. You're not yourself." Alas, where James's contemporaries didn't comprehend his first statement, they *butchered* the meaning of his second: "We are making use of only a small part of our possible mental and physical resources."

In a tragic game of broken telephone that spans a century, James's concluding remark evolved (or devolved) to give life to the myth that we utilize only 10% of our brain's capacity. But James wasn't talking about the brain's *physiological* potential; he was talking about the development of the *psyche*. While the symptoms he described remained misunderstood and thus ignored, the underlying ailment festered.

Just as you don't want a history lesson, we don't want to bore you with statistics either. Lest we underestimate the magnitude of the problem, though, the somber folks at Gallup point out that a full two-thirds of workers are unengaged at work. And that number has been constant for the past twenty years.[2]

But the workplace is just a small representation of a much more worrying trend. People are quiet quitting all aspects of their lives. In his psychology practice in Menlo Park, California, Rom helps clients who, simply put, have lost some of their spark.

If you met any of these people walking down the street, you wouldn't be able to pick out anything specifically wrong with them. But when they sit down in Rom's office for the first time, they share, for example, that they've become so pessimistic about finding the ideal romantic partner that they've settled for someone who's "meh." Or they are so weighed down by the daily grind that they don't pepper their lives with exciting adventures. Their fires are damped, their drafts are checked. That is, they live their lives in a sort of low-flame mode.

The field of psychology in general has little to offer these people beyond Band-Aid solutions: focus on the positive, keep a gratitude journal, be more mindful, etc.

We can't completely blame psychologists; they have their hands full with people in various degrees of acute crisis. The field has extensive treatment plans for individuals who, for example, feel so sad that they can't get out of bed, or so anxious they can't leave the house: cognitive behavioral therapy, insight-oriented therapy, group therapy, and more.

But come to a psychologist's office and ask how you can thrive, how your psyche can be at its full potential, and you're likely to catch your therapist off guard and may even get a blank stare.

That's because in its infancy, psychology abounded with theories about why people struggled. They ranged from the personal to the familial. Some were esoteric or outlandish, delving into the realms of far-fetched myths or even sexual energy.

The psychiatrist Aaron Beck found himself lost among these theories and instead took a pragmatic approach: rather than trying to explain *why* someone became, say, depressed, he decided, we should try to understand how a depressed person sees the world and then proceed from there.

He constructed an inventory that captures the experience of a depressed person, with self-ratings ranging from "I do not feel sad" to "I am so sad and unhappy that I can't stand it." That inventory unintentionally focuses psychologists on a truncated segment of the spectrum: people whose flames are nearly extinguished. But surely there's more to life than simply not feeling sad?

If you have children (or if you don't, imagine that you do), isn't your goal for them to live life so that they are so happy they can't wait to jump out of bed in the morning? Don't you want them not to settle for low-flame mode but to embrace a state of being that can only be described as "wow"?

As a psychologist, Rom has that goal for each and every client. When someone presents with a low-burning flame, he asks himself: What would it take to turn this person not just into someone who isn't suffering but into someone who is feeling *wow* about their life? What would it look like for this person to operate in full-flame mode?

It's amazing how people lose sight of what they love, like creating art or staying up late with friends or attending concerts or traveling. The point isn't just to do one or two or three of these things. The point is to shift gears and live a life that prioritizes and optimizes for them. The clients who embrace this approach undergo a transformation so fundamental and so extreme that they become unrecognizable. *Literally*.

One of the first times Rom saw it was early in his career when he was walking on a college campus and heard someone call out his name. Looking around and seeing no faces he recognized, he assumed he must have misheard "Ron." But then he heard it again, "Rom," unmistakable this time. The third time he heard it, he spotted the young woman calling out to him, but even looking her right in the face he wasn't able to place her.

Only when she started talking did it hit him that this was a client he had seen only two weeks ago. She had first come in three months earlier, saying she was single, had a history of being in subpar relationships, and was pessimistic about ever finding the right person. Her energy was subdued, her eyes tired.

But now, three months later, she looked like an entirely different person. Her eyes were radiant and so piercing they seemed to look right to your core. She had the confidence of a diplomat and the poise of a duchess. She was grounded and so strikingly alive that her energy seemed to burst forth from within. Somehow a switch had been flipped.

It wasn't that any of the factors causing her difficulties had changed. She had not found the partner of her dreams or even started dating someone she was enthusiastic about. Rather, she was able to look at the world and herself through a different lens.

Her flame was fully alight. Rom has seen over and over again that getting to that spot requires shedding the mundane and developing an almost allergic reaction to everything that feels emotionally heavy and uninspiring. Over the years, when we've seen people exhibit this full flame across various disciplines, it's always caught our attention.

"In the world we live in, ninety-eight percent of what gets built and designed today is pure shit," Frank Gehry declared to a group of reporters in Spain. "There's no sense of design nor respect for humanity or anything."[3]

We had to ask ourselves, why would a world-renowned architect have such an overblown reaction to ordinary buildings? To get to the answer, we need to go back to long before he designed any buildings, to his earliest, most vulnerable memories.

When we spoke with Gehry, he opened up about a life-changing event that happened when he was in elementary school.

"I grew up in a Canadian mining town," he told us. "I was enrolled in an elementary school where anti-Semitism was the rule of the day. I was beaten up often. It went on for five years."

One specific incident from that period stands out in his mind. Another child was celebrating his birthday, and everyone was invited out to the schoolyard to sing "Happy Birthday." Everyone, that is, except Gehry. "I was told to stay inside," he remembered.

Whether the teachers were trying to protect or to punish Gehry is still not clear to him. But he had a sort of out-of-body experience. He was able to view himself as separate from the school. And once he disassociated himself in that way, he was able to see and question the inner workings of the machine. He developed an antipathy to the rote and factory-like nature of school, an aversion that stayed with him through-out his professional career.

As he explained to us, "I don't think I'm more different than any-one else. It's a matter of questioning and curiosity." That's exactly why he got so furious at the other 98% of architects: they have the training and ability to do great things, but they go about their business in a fog, choosing not to.

Interestingly, Gehry has the same sort of disdain for the system that quiet quitters do. He could easily have figured, "Most architecture is ordinary, and I don't like the ordinary, so I'll just check out and go through the motions." But instead, he switched gears and became engaged in a way that felt authentic and meaningful, just like Rom's unrecognizable client. Gehry became one of the world's best-known and most lauded architects, designing whimsical and wildly creative buildings like the Dancing House in Prague and the Guggenheim Museum Bilbao.

The problem is that quiet quitters reduce their options to a false dichotomy: either get with the program and be productive or be on the fringes and resist. Gehry found the third gear: Don't get with the mun-dane program *nor* drag your feet. Instead, rise above them both.

It's easy, though, to find yourself settling or going with the status quo because it's the path of least resistance. Take Pietro Leemann of Joia in Milan. A classically trained chef who studied in Europe and Asia, he could easily have pursued a career cooking traditional food.

But Leemann was intrigued by the vegetarian way of living and wanted to create food that was both sublime and healthy. The con-straints he imposed on himself—vegetarian food and a healthy menu—became a way of differentiating himself from the crowd. His restaurant, Joia, became the first vegetarian restaurant in the world to receive a Michelin star.

When we talked to Leemann about the plant-based food trend, his expression soured. "With Beyond Meat or Impossible Foods . . . the society follows a fashion, but they're not nice to eat; they're actually terrible to eat. The reality is that the food should reflect the purity that every person has inside. We should wake up the purity of the people." This idea of purity is Leeman's internal North Star.

What's most interesting about Gehry and Leemann is that they both have a certain quality that we don't even have a word for: They don't want to simply check a box. They have a clarity of purpose that guides them to a life that is, for lack of a better word, *wow*.

This *wow* state is not just for world-renowned chefs and architects. We can all get there, not only at work but in every part of our lives. Here are some first steps on the path to *wow*:

1. What do you wake up in the morning feeling super-excited about? If the answer is "not much," start keeping a mental list of the things you do feel excited about and make it a priority to incorporate them into your life.

2. Which people in your life energize you and make you feel fully alive? Maximize the amount of time you spend with them. Let them know how great it is to be around them.

3. What activities resonate with you and bring out your best self? What does your energized best self look like in those moments? Get to know that part of you because that's your core strength.

4. When something feels heavy, negative, or draining, pay attention to that feeling. But don't just walk away or quiet quit. Instead, ask yourself: What can I do to turn this into something that will feel incredible?

Stop quiet quitting your life. Always, always go for *wow*.

Biographies

Ori Brafman is an internationally renowned *New York Times*–bestselling author and a distinguished teaching fellow at UC Berkeley's Haas School of Business. His books include *The Starfish and the Spider: The Unstoppable Power of Leaderless Organizations*; *Radical Inclusion: What the Post-9/11 World Should Have Taught Us About Leadership*; and *Sway: The Irresistible Pull of Irrational Behavior*. In 2022, he was named to the Thinkers50 Radar list of up-and-coming thinkers whose ideas could make a positive difference in the world.

Rom Brafman holds a PhD in psychology and has taught university courses in personality and personal growth. His research focuses on the dynamics of interpersonal relationships. He has a private practice in Palo Alto, California. He is the co-author (with Ori Brafman) of *Sway: The Irresistible Pull of Irrational Behavior.*

Notes

1. William James, "The Energies of Men," *Philosophical Review* 16(1) (January 1907): 1–20.
2. Jim Harter, "Is Quiet Quitting Real?," Gallup, September 6, 2022, www .gallup.com/workplace/398306/quiet-quitting-real.aspx.
3. Luis Martinez, "La peineta del arquitecto," *El Mundo*, October 23, 2014.

16

Policy

The Path to Prevent Burnout

Jennifer Moss

After years of facing a confluence of health and economic fears, rapid societal shifts, environmental threats, and political dissonance, it makes sense that global mental health is on the decline. Combine this lack of personal well-being with chronic workplace stress and you've got a workforce ripe for burnout. An unhealthy stew created by the pandemic, now at its boiling point.

And despite a desire to push all of this burnout talk into the background, it still requires more conversation. For example, a recent study of 10,000 knowledge-based workers in seven different countries found that 70% experienced burnout in 2022. Healthcare hit peak levels of burnout—higher than any other sector. A study of 4,467 nurses found that 94% were experiencing burnout. Physician burnout is 1.7 times higher than it was pre-pandemic and suicidal ideation increased by 1.5 times (14% of the 4,121 physicians surveyed).

Before the crisis, in 2019, burnout was defined by the World Health Organization (WHO) as "a syndrome conceptualized as resulting from chronic workplace stress that has not been successfully managed. It is characterized by three dimensions:

- feelings of energy depletion or exhaustion;
- increased mental distance from one's job, or feelings of negativism or cynicism related to one's job; and
- reduced professional efficacy."[1]

However, this particular crisis was more pronounced than others. It has left a permanent mark. Since the pandemic was so global, and all at once, and yet ruthlessly enduring, it shook the world and exploded the workforce. It highlighted that work as we understand it simply isn't working and maybe never has.

So, what's going on?

The first hit came when the labor force went into lockdown. When employers realized that the pandemic wasn't an acute crisis like a flood or a fire, they scrambled to figure out a plan. Nothing was quick and easy. The vacuum effect of sickness and layoffs and a backlog of work to tackle meant that the workforce rebooted more like a Commodore 64 than a MacBook Air.

The second hit came as women were forced to exit the labor force in dramatic numbers. Women lost approximately 5.4 million net jobs in the early months of the pandemic. The addition of 15–20 more hours of unpaid labor each week caused an exodus of women from the labor force. Data from the International Labour Organization (ILO) in 2022 show that two million moms are no longer participating in the global workforce.

The third punch came in waves of resignations. In 2021, according to the U.S. Bureau of Labor Statistics, over 47 million Americans voluntarily quit their jobs. Today, it's estimated that four million people are out of work due to long Covid with an annual cost of $170 billion a year in lost wages.

With attrition at its peak, the remaining staff took on unsustainable workloads, many adding an average of 2.5 hours to their workday. The fourth hit came in response to burnout spreading rampantly across the workforce. It initiated the quiet quitting phenomenon, a pejorative term that doesn't address the problem in any real way because quitting isn't a privilege everyone can afford.

At this point, the workforce is in survival mode. Someone needed to stop and shout, "It's not urgent! We're not in an emergency anymore! It's just an email!" And, yet, in a great many organizations there was silence.

The fifth strike came as employers started to insist employees "go back to work" (as if they had been "away" from work). Depersonalized mass emails sent out to say that everyone needs to be back in the office—or else. In 2022, resignation data remained unchanged. According to Microsoft Trends data, people say they're quitting for these three big reasons:

1. Lack of empathy from employer or manager.
2. Unsustainable workload.
3. Lack of development and training.

This isn't an exhaustive list. These are the highlights—or perhaps better to say the lowlights—of the last few years. There was already a storm brewing long before the crisis hit. But not every crisis has to end in disaster. In a post-traumatic growth moment, the ship rights itself and tracks a new course.

Analyzing what happened is a critical first step. After that it's all about, "what now?"

When the Tank Empties

Let's start with the physiological impact.

Amishi Jha, neuroscientist and Associate Professor of Psychology at the University of Miami, shares that volatility, uncertainty, complexity, and ambiguity (VUCA for short) takes a serious toll on mental health.

Uncertainty in short bursts can be healthy. It develops skills like emotional flexibility and cognitive optimism. The capacity to quickly pivot and take a new approach to solving a problem increases confidence and risk tolerance. Yielding to these traits also develops stronger, more resilient leadership capabilities. So far, so good.

However, prolonged uncertainty, as in the case of a multi-year crisis brought on by the pandemic, can be emotionally and mentally catastrophic.

"Attention is the brain's superpower but threat, stress, and poor mood will rapidly degrade [its] capacities," Jha explains. "COVID is producing circumstances that accelerate the rate at which attention is degraded."[2]

With the pandemic stressors impacting working memory, attention is now focused on "policing instincts and behaviors, as well as overcoming impulses and habits." All of this "sucks up limited attention and finite working memory capacity, leaving few cognitive resources for anything else," says Jha.

Across organizations, attention degradation has become a liability. Employees and leaders alike describe brain fog, a psychological term that shows up in symptoms that include: atypical mistakes, difficulty making simple decisions, poor recall, and a self-reported "fuzziness" in the brain that reduces effectiveness and motivation.

Even more challenging during the crisis was the prevailing "business as usual" attitude. Hitting pre-pandemic goals was already hard for an increasingly burned-out workforce. But being asked to remain in high-growth mode while pivoting on the fly made it unsustainable for many. This was worsened by the fact that symptoms of burnout and brain fog were often misdiagnosed as underperformance.

For employers, there is a point where one must pause and assess the sustainability of it all. Instead of a strategy that includes losing and hiring back half the workforce (again), what if the near future of work was all about recovery: a strategy that reallocates resources to rehabilitate those who are unwell instead of shuffling through those who are sick? Start by reducing overwork, increasing fairness and justice, bringing back learning and development to pre-pandemic levels, rebuilding community?

It is *really* that radical!

Prioritizing Psychological Safety

In 1784, a fever outbreak among cotton mill workers in the United Kingdom led to the Health and Morals of Apprentices Act in 1802. The Act required factories to provide proper ventilation and clean workspaces.

It would take another 216 years before mental health at work laws were installed. Ontario in Canada would be the first in the world to establish these laws. In 2000, the Human Rights at Work section became part of the Ontario Human Rights Code (the Code).[3]

Then, in 2013, Canada was once again the first in the world to establish a national mental health at work strategy referred to as the National Standard of Canada for Psychological Health and Safety in the Workplace.[4] It gained enormous interest internationally and became the standard by which other countries model.

It would be another 7 years before the pandemic triggered a slew of global leaders to start enacting their own policies. The rationale may be in response to a dramatic rise in mental health claims in 2020. Although insurers say "hold on" as they predict a "tsunami" of claims to come in the years ahead.

Firms around the world are recognizing the shocking cost of mental illness. Global estimates by the World Health Organization (WHO) claim 12 billion working days are lost every year to depression and anxiety at a cost of US$1 trillion per year in decreased productivity. In Canada, the economic impact of poor employee mental health is estimated at $50 billion annually. In the US, that figure is $300 billion.

In 2022, the WHO and the U.S. Surgeon General came out with new standards on mental health in the workplace. For many this has felt like a long time coming. As Canada and Australia have been leading the way for years, the pandemic pushed policy-makers to react more forcefully.

The Frameworks to Follow

The WHO Guidelines on Mental Health at Work is a highly detailed and well-researched global framework.[5] At 134 pages, the guide offers robust recommendations to promote mental health and prevent mental illness at work. It covers "organizational interventions, manager training and worker training, individual interventions, return to work, and gaining employment."

The U.S. Surgeon General's Framework for Mental Health & Well-Being in the Workplace[6] is more scaled down but highly accessible, making it easy for organizations to adopt and operationalize.

The framework has five pillars with a focus at the center on worker voice and equity. The five pillars are:

1. Protection from Harm
   - Prioritize workplace physical and psychological safety
   - Enable adequate rest
   - Normalize and support mental health
   - Operationalize DEIA[7] norms, policies, and programs

2. Work-Life Harmony
   - Provide more autonomy over how work is done
   - Make schedules as flexible and predictable as possible
   - Increase access to paid leave
   - Respect boundaries between work and non-work time

3. Mattering at Work
   - Provide a living wage
   - Engage workers in workplace decisions
   - Build a culture of gratitude and recognition
   - Connect individual work with organizational mission

4. Connection and Community
   - Create cultures of inclusion and belonging
   - Cultivate trusted relationships
   - Foster collaboration and teamwork

5. Opportunity for Growth
   - Offer quality training, education, and mentoring
   - Foster clear, equitable pathways for career advancement
   - Ensure relevant, reciprocal feedback

There are myriad tactics to perform under these goals and those efforts will vary from one organization to another. "Ensuring workplace well-being requires an intentional, ongoing effort by employers and leaders across all levels, with the voices of workers and more equitable policy and practice environment at the center," says Dr. Murthy, the Surgeon General.[8]

For example, under the second pillar, Work-Life Harmony, where it states, "respect boundaries between work and non-work time," consider a Right to Disconnect Policy. A law that prohibits employers from making their employees work outside of designated work hours. This followed on the heels of France which founded the law in 2016 and other countries like Canada, Germany, Italy, the Philippines, and Slovakia following suit.

Another example, under the fourth pillar, Connection and Community, "foster collaboration and teamwork," considers shared versus individual goals, get togethers for work sprints, encouraging turn taking in meetings, having non-work-related check-ins that focus on active listening and fun. Having one best friend at work reduces burnout by 41%, making connection and community an essential part of a burnout prevention strategy.

Under the first pillar, Protection from Harm, "enable adequate rest," it's critical for leaders to reduce workload. Overwork is the leading cause of burnout and responsible for the death of 700,000 people annually. It's a serious consequence of long working hours. The WHO considers anything over 55 hours per week as overworking.

One of the ways to enable rest is to reduce meeting fatigue. According to Microsoft Trends data, Teams meetings alone have increased by 252%. Create a culture where it's OK to decline meetings and for hosts to invite only necessary participants.

Look at Dr. Dalton Smith's work related to rest. She believes that humans are experiencing a global rest deficit and suggests everyone requires seven types of rest to be at their best. It's worth noting that bringing the concept of self-care into the workforce is a good intention. However, if employees perceive that they don't have the time and support to engage in self-care, then the intention is sure to fail. Make time. Model time.

Most importantly, the way to succeed in reducing burnout and improving mental health at work is to lead with empathy. Ask questions and take action on the answers. With so much rapid change and uncertainty, being present, agile, and responsive makes the right kind of leader for these times.

I believe, however, that we're righting the pendulum. According to Dialectical Behavior Theory, two things can be true at the same time. The pandemic was and still is one of the most challenging collective crises to affect the world. Also true, the pandemic has built an emotionally flexible, resilient, and transformational workforce that is finally making mental health a priority.

Labeling hardships and their effects—both the good and the bad—moves us all forward. And yet, we struggle to take learning into action. To build a healthy future of work, we need to encode those healthy behaviors today. Without a framework, we're all just feeling our way through the dark. Policy won't solve all the challenges we're facing. But, right now it's the light switch we need to turn on.

Biography

Jennifer Moss is an award-winning journalist, author, and international public speaker. She is the author of *The Burnout Epidemic: The Rise of Chronic Stress and How We Can Fix It;* and *Unlocking Happiness at Work* in 2022, she was named to the Thinkers50 Radar list of up-and-coming thinkers whose ideas could make a positive difference in the world.

Notes

1. WHO, https://www.who.int/news/item/28-05-2019-burn-out-an-occupational-phenomenon-international-classification-of-diseases.
2. Amishi Jha, https://amishi.com/.
3. Ontario Human Rights Code, https://www.ohrc.on.ca/en/ontario-human-rights-code
4. https://www.mentalhealthcommission.ca/national-standard
5. WHO Guidelines on Mental Health at Work, https://www.who.int/publications-detail-redirect/. . .
6. U.S. Surgeon General's Framework for Mental Health & Well-Being in the Workplace, https://www.aha.org/news/headline/2022-10-21-surgeon-general-releases-framework-workplace-mental-health-well-being.
7. DEIA = diversity, equity, inclusion, and accessibility.
8. Ibid.

IV

Voices of Difference

17

Voices of Difference at Work

Megan Reitz

One thing is for certain when things are *un*certain. When we face "wicked" challenges that defy easy solutions—such as how to keep talented employees, respond to left-field shifts in social expectations, or change our strategy to engage with the realities of climate change—we need to have some seriously good conversations. That's the only way to take wise and unfamiliar action.

One could surmise that "good" here would include the ability to hear multiple perspectives that really challenge (and disturb) traditional ways of thinking and doing, and that engage with ideas that may or may not work in practice—where we seek to learn from mistakes and failures without spiraling down into blame games.

Conversations that are only influenced by and only include the opinions of those who are high in traditional status and authority will be doomed to failure, unless of course those individuals possess the remarkable capacity to see and experience the world from all angles.

This is one reason why we hear most of those who are in perceived positions of power asking those who aren't to speak up, and why HR departments are focusing so keenly on developing psychological safety. Without voices of difference, ethical conduct, innovation, inclusion, and engagement—and therefore performance—are illusive.

For the last decade, my research partner, John Higgins, and I have been exploring the choices employees make around whether to speak up or stay silent—and whether to listen or ignore. We are particularly interested in the reasons why leaders' efforts to encourage speaking up so frequently fail, why employee surveys persistently return poor ratings in the "I feel able to speak up" category, and why reported levels of workplace engagement in the annual global Gallup survey remain so anemic.

Here, I'll go through three common mistakes we see leaders making, and then I'll explore how we might create and then navigate spaces for dialogue inside the organizational (and societal) systems that so desperately need them.

Mistake #1: Trying to Fix the Silent People

In the very first case study at the start of our research, we were told by a senior leader that employees needed to be more courageous and assertive. A cascade of "how to speak up" workshops was apparently their preferred solution. When we talked with employees, one told us that "last time someone spoke up round here, they disappeared."

We commonly point the finger at people who are silent and tell them to speak up. We'd be far better off developing our capacity to listen and to create a system where employees feel safe to speak up. "Why should they," we said to this particular leader, "need to be so courageous in the first place?"

Speaking up is relational. It happens more easily in response to someone we feel is genuinely inviting us to speak up on our own terms, and then listening in a way that means we are likely to speak up again. Therefore, while I'm all for the speak-up workshops, I'd prioritize the listen-up ones for managers and leaders.

Mistake #2: Trying to Avoid the P Word

While there are many notable and useful skills that can be taught around speaking up and listening up, their effectiveness will be limited if our construction of power, status, and authority remains the same.

To explain, we label ourselves and others all the time—gender, ethnicity, hierarchy, age, department, location, tenure, education, language . . . you name it, we label it. These labels help us to understand our relative status in different contexts. And if there's one thing that determines our choices on whether we can or should speak up, and whether it is likely that we will be listened to, it's perceptions of power and who has it and who doesn't.

So, if you want to change who says what and who gets heard, you have to disrupt perceptions of power. The problem is that many of us find it awkward talking about power. If we are the person in power, we may well want to keep it and we're often not even aware of the consequences our labels have on others' voices.

So, it's a "get real" moment. Do you *really* want others to have more power in this system? How are you going to elevate their status relative to yours to invite genuine dialogue? What work do you need to do on yourself to own the messiness of your own personal and cultural history and all the taken-for-granted attitudes about others you've never really had to face up to (beyond saying what someone else has advised you are the right words to parade in public)?

Mistake #3: Asking People to Bring Their Whole Selves to Work . . . Except for the Tricky Bits

A finance director I spoke with recently confided that he'd asked his team to speak up primarily hoping for "more transparency over compliance issues and a few good ideas." After his team eventually heeded his invitation for them to "bring their whole selves to work" by raising issues of race, gender, and climate change, he admitted he "hadn't banked on getting everything else."

The rise in employee activism and the desire by employees to speak about wider environmental and societal issues have tested "speak up" initiatives to the limit and left many looking like they were simply bandwagon projects. If you ask employees to speak up, then you need to be ready to have some conversations that you may not feel comfortable with and you may not be practiced in. For white, senior leaders in the Global North, for example, having conversations about ethnicity and race can feel like a minefield.

To summarize, if you navigate these common mistakes, then creating spaces for dialogue and developing psychological safety require you to be able to *inquire* into what matters to your stakeholders, *facilitate* conversations comprising multiple perspectives, and *act* in a way that helps conversations to continue, rather than ignoring the complexity of the situation, collapsing it into your own worldview, or reaching out for the easiest and most obvious solution to hand.

Let's look at these three areas now.

Inquire

Inquiry relies on us seeking out others' views with genuine curiosity and noticing our judgments as we do that.

We won't inquire if we already think we know what people have to say. Data from our research suggest that the more senior we are, the more we are likely to overestimate the degree to which people are speaking up to us. On top of that, we are likely to overestimate how approachable we are and how good we are at listening. All this means that we are in an "optimism bubble"—we think people are telling us what we need to hear. But they aren't. We are far more disconnected than we realize, and we won't inquire well unless we accept that we are in a bubble and need to do a lot more work to reach out and listen.

We won't inquire if we think others agree. Without getting too deeply into the world of linguistics, the one rule of thumb all managers and leaders should live by is that what you say never has the same meaning as what was heard—in other words, you can't make sense on someone else's behalf, and if what you say is met by polite nods or silence, that doesn't tell you a thing about what has actually landed with people.

And we won't inquire if we've already discounted certain voices. In our recent research on employee activism, we asked thousands of people what the label "activist" conjured up for them. Turns out that if you're known as an "activist," you may be perceived to be a purpose-driven, passionate change-agent, or an aggressive, rebellious troublemaker. Of course, if you're an employee activist, how you are perceived by your manager will clearly shape whether they will listen to you, as well as the consequences you will face if you challenge the status quo.

If we are to genuinely find out our blind spots and hear views contrary to our own, we have to be aware of the judgments we hold about the other person. If we don't, we risk overinflating some voices and deleting others.

Facilitate

The word "dialogue" is used a lot in organizations. It often has a somewhat cozy, warm feel to it. But being "in dialogue" can be far more bracing than that. Dialogue means we are voicing difference. It means we are entering into territory that we probably haven't been in before and we don't know where it is going. And that means we're probably in for a bumpy ride where there are disagreements, misunderstandings, mistakes, and fallout. The very things that leaders and managers tend to avoid, often because they are felt to be inefficient or may paint them in a bad light.

If we invite dialogue, we cannot then rush to consensus. Of course, that doesn't mean we let all hell break loose. It's appropriate to have rules of engagement—time given to hear views, showing respect and appreciation—and potentially boundaries around when decisions have to be made, when you as a senior person are going to use the authority and power that your position gives you.

If we want employees to be able to enter into dialogue, then the way leaders role-model this ability to disagree and make mistakes (or not) is fundamental. I have seen too many leaders tell their teams to challenge one another and respect divergent views, but then either desperately attempt to show uniform beliefs and perfection in the leadership team or end up role-modeling utter dysfunction instead, having competitive battles between departments which employees are only too aware of.

Act

If inquiring and facilitating dialogue aren't perceived to lead to action, then people may eventually give up. They'll roll their eyes when they're invited to speak up and say: "What's the point?"

We coined the phrase "façadism" in our research—it describes the situation when leaders make statements (such as many did after George Floyd's murder regarding race equity) but then don't act. They say the right thing, but it is a façade.

Sometimes there's a lack of action because busyness gets in the way. Sometimes there was never any real commitment in the first place. Either way, the effect can be devastating as employees withdraw their thoughts and ideas because "What's the point?" And it can then take a very long time to turn this situation around—to persuade employees that there is a point.

We can't act on everything. Organizations and their leaders can't take a stand on every issue. However, they do need to make choices on what to pursue and what not to. Especially in relation to activist issues, sitting on the fence is as dangerous now as getting off it and so what you need to do is to have a coherent, thoughtful process in place, in which you sift through, with stakeholders, what you'll act on and what you won't.

Circling back, this process must have robust methods of inquiry to find out what really matters to stakeholders, and then dialogue, which shares information and decision-making to direct meaningful action.

Closing Thoughts

Leading at times of great uncertainty requires fantastic conversations which share ideas and challenge the status quo. We all know that. That's why leaders ask employees to speak up.

But when leaders ask this of others, do they realize the implications, or is their invitation a thinly disguised veneer over the old (but still popular) story of "good" leadership, where someone in power knows the answer and convinces others to follow?

A newer story is about leaders who know their perspective on something is partial—sometimes very partial—and so, with curiosity, they reach out to find out their blind spots, making decisions with others.

That's a very different story. That involves a very different leadership practice which might well sit uncomfortably with the practices that people have been selected, promoted, and rewarded for in the past. It's time to buckle up because leadership is going to be in for a bumpy ride—but one which has the potential to be more personally and collectively satisfying while delivering organizational performance that is fit for the wider purposes demanded by the age we are living through.

Biography

Megan Reitz is Professor of Leadership and Dialogue at Hult International Business School and founder of Reitz Consulting. She is an internationally recognized expert on speaking truth to power and employee activism, and the author of *Speak Up: Say What Needs to Be Said and Hear What Needs to Be Heard*. In 2017, she was named to the Thinkers50 Radar list of up-and-coming thinkers whose ideas could make a positive difference in the world, and in 2021 she was ranked among the 50 most influential management thinkers in the world.

18

Want More Female Leaders? Develop Leadership When It Matters Most

Julie Carrier

Ella* took a deep breath. It was time. She was a special guest on a global podcast by Thinkers50, the world's most reliable resource for identifying, ranking, and sharing the leading management ideas of our age.[1] She was ready. Along with the president of her organization, she expertly engaged with Des Dearlove, co-founder of Thinkers50, sharing her personal experiences with a groundbreaking, evidence-based leader development and coaching program that had radically transformed not only her life but the lives of many of her colleagues.

It was hard to believe that just a few months ago, Ella was terrified of public speaking and so shy she wouldn't speak up or talk in group settings. Now, here she was, radiating confidence and self-awareness and speaking with authority. Ella credits the program for helping her to grow as a leader—so much so, that she says colleagues from her previous organization would not recognize her.

---

*Names of the girls have been changed to maintain confidentiality.

Inspired by Amy Edmondson's groundbreaking work on psychological safety, Emmaline* led her high-performing team to finish their Leadership Team Charter—a powerful living document and a formal agreement that outlines their leadership team's purpose, their goals, and their norms. The Charter supports the core tenets of Edmonson's work—ensuring the team is a safe place to speak up, ask questions, learn, grow, and, crucially, make mistakes.[2] After some intense collaboration, they completed their Charter, signed it, and displayed it prominently in their meeting room.

The team intentionally reviews the Charter each week together to ensure mutual support and accountability. Before coming to this organization, Emmaline used to dread team projects and meetings—but now she finds them to be some of the most meaningful parts of her day. Even more, instead of fearing failures or mistakes as roadblocks, Emmaline and her team now celebrate them as stepping stones to successful outcomes.

Sherise* is a caring, powerful, and authentic leader in her organization. The junior team is in awe of her. Her confidence, emotional intelligence, and leadership presence inspire them to believe that someday they can have her leadership capability, too. In everything she does and says to them, Sherise demonstrates a new model of leadership that is collaborative and character-based—and one that begins with self-leadership, based on the principle that the first person you must lead is yourself.

No one would have guessed that, just a year ago, Sherise didn't see herself as a leader. Instead, she felt alone and purposeless and faced challenges with some of her colleagues. Then, through participating in a leader development program, she realized, "Leadership is not a title or position—it is a choice." She *chose to lead herself* and that changed everything. Now she is inspiring everyone else to do the same. She had gone from being one of the biggest critics of her organization to one of its biggest champions.

What is this organization? Who are these leaders? How have they accomplished such extraordinary leadership outcomes?

I'll give you a hint. This organization is not on Fortune's list of "100 Best Companies to Work For." It is not an acclaimed startup in

---

* Names have been changed to maintain confidentiality.

Silicon Valley or a global NGO. The leaders in these true stories are not 20-somethings, 30-somethings or even senior executives.

They are 14-year-old girls who attend St. Ursula Academy high school in Toledo, Ohio.

This is what happens when we bring the power of world-class leadership coaching and evidence-based leader development—normally reserved for the C-Suite—to impact young women during one of the most formative times of their development, high school.

This is the future of education—and it is not just an idea, it is happening now.

Each of these students participates in The Leadership Course™, an innovative, four-year, evidence-based, applied neuroscience leader development program for high school girls. Strongly supported by school leadership, it is taught as part of the academic school day by certified in-school leadership coaches. The program is the result of years of careful design, pilot testing, and rigorous evaluation and development, leveraging cutting-edge best practices in leader development, educational neuroscience, and positive and social psychology.

It is advised and developed by a team of the world's foremost thought leaders in coaching and leader development from Harvard, the United States Military Academy at West Point, the Center on Leadership and Ethics at the Fuqua School of Business at Duke University, the Doerr Institute for New Leaders at Rice University and the Kellogg School of Management at Northwestern University, along with many others. With the support of Thinkers50, Marshall Goldsmith and other renowned thought leaders, schools, parents, and the students themselves, The Leadership Course™ helps to expand the paradigm of traditional leader development and coaching to impact the next generation. More, it broadens the scope of what secondary education can be—by closing the gender confidence and leadership gap and resulting in dramatic increases in leader identity, resilience, and even academic performance for underserved students.

In fact, through rigorous evaluation, the program was found to result in statistically significant increases in self-efficacy and growth mindset for participants—factors that highly correlate with greater motivation, learning, and performance.[3]

As a direct result of the program, data show that among the girls in the program:[4]

- 85% report an increase in confidence;
- 90% report their leadership skills improved;
- 90% feel more connected to their peers;
- 95% report they are better able to work with others as a team.

Some 100% of the leadership coaches (certified in-school faculty and educators) find it so personally meaningful to their lives inside and outside the classroom, that they elect to continue to facilitate The Leadership Course™, as part of their full course-load of other classes.

Approximately 90% of students say they would recommend the program to others.

With an ever increasingly complex and rapidly changing world, the time has come to take a long-lens perspective on leader development.[5] We must stop viewing leadership development and coaching as the exclusive purview of adults and must begin developing leaders when it matters most—adolescence.

Why? *Two words: Leader identity.*

Leader Identity

Research confirms that leadership doesn't start in adulthood—it starts in childhood—more specifically, during the teen years.[6] Leader identity, the ability to see oneself as a leader, is one of the most crucial and most overlooked aspects of leader development, both in adolescence and adulthood.[7]

Because people tend to live in alignment with their self-concept, organizations can spend millions teaching about leadership, but without a strong leader identity, individuals will be less likely to use those leadership skills and competencies, apply for that promotion or seek out opportunities to lead.[8] Simply put, you can teach people leadership skills, but if they don't *see* themselves as leaders, they likely won't use them.

On the other hand, having a strong "leader identity" impacts a whole range of other beliefs and behaviors. Those with strong leader identities feel more confident to lead when opportunities arise; have the desire to pursue (and do pursue) leadership roles; are able to stand up for personal convictions and voice opinions even if they are unpopular; and act in ways that are consistent with their values and core beliefs.[9]

When does leader identity formation start? Adolescence. The traditional model of leadership development and coaching as the exclusive purview of adults misses the mark for the most formative, significant, and crucial times of leader development based on human development and neuroscience research.

Adolescence is an unprecedented time for learning, growth, and development in which youth "identities and potential are being profoundly and rapidly influenced and shaped, including their development of a leadership identity."[10]

This is important because neuroscience research shows that adolescence is a time of exceptional neuroplasticity and brain development.[11] In fact, an adolescent's self-concept, skills and beliefs practiced during this time help to develop the *hardwired* physical neural connections for their adult brain.[12] Leader development and coaching for adolescents equip young people to hard-code leader identity—as well as success-oriented and pro-social traits, such as self-confidence, growth mindset, grit, self-awareness, comfort with public speaking, strengths awareness, purpose development, and many other skills for adulthood—leveraging this formative time and rare window of exponential growth and leader identity formation.

Don't students just naturally develop leader identity as a byproduct of their academic education? No.

Research has found that when a student engages in an academic-only curriculum this results in approximately a 0% increase student leader identity.[13] When students engage in evidence-based leader development and coaching, however, they have significant increases in leader identity.[14]

This makes sense. We would not expect a student who has *never* attended a calculus class to automatically know *advanced math skills*. The same is true for leadership. Leader identity and leadership skills are *learned competencies*. Leadership must be taught, and taught the right way—and begin at the right time. That time is high school.

How? In secondary education, leader development must be more than just an afterthought or a school mission statement. It must be curricular. Just like students go to math, science, and English classes, they should be able to go to their applied-neuroscience leadership class. Based on our research, it must integrate these four core elements:

1. **High school leader development must focus on helping students cultivate a leader identity:** Rather than just learning about leadership, leader development programs must focus on helping students *see themselves as leaders*. To do this, schools must leverage educational neuroscience—and break with the traditional lecture-only academic paradigm. Leadership starts with self-awareness, self-knowledge, and self-leadership that cannot be directly taught, but that can be developed and experienced through active learning, facilitation, and leadership coaching. Prior to facilitating the program, educators must be thoughtfully selected and receive professional training or certification in ontological coaching approaches to leader development.

2. **High school leader development must highlight a character-based leadership model:** Rather than outdated top-down and command and control perspectives on leadership, leader development should focus on a model of leadership that is character-based, collaborative, and non-hierarchical—the model needed for our increasingly challenging and complex world. This must then be supported with structured opportunities for students to apply their leadership skills and be recognized and rewarded for their character and contributions beyond academic outcomes and test scores.

3. **High school leader development programs must be evidence-based and rigorously evaluated:**[15] Leader development in high school deserves the same level of substance and intentionality as leader development in high performing organizations. Rather than in-house, ad-hoc approaches, the leadership curriculum (pedagogy, framework, and exercises) should be evidence-based, rooted in neuroscience, and leverage current findings in leader development

research. As an example from The Leadership Course™, one short 30-minute writing reflection exercise is supported by over 190 published studies.[16] Programs must also be evaluated beyond standard student participation metrics. Evaluations must be rigorous and include the use of valid and reliable assessments to ensure learning effectiveness.

4. **High school leader development must be for *all* students:** Leader development should be an integrated and intentional part of the academic school day—making it equitable and accessible to *all students*. In our research, we find that the students who grow the most are the ones who, because of outdated social narratives and gendered leadership stereotypes, often start off least seeing themselves as leaders, especially girls and young women. Previous research supports those observations.[17] Leadership classes or opportunities should not be reserved for the prized few whose privilege or support have already provided them the space to cultivate a leader identity to self-select these developmental experiences. They should be provided to all students—and not as an option. Just like other graded, core classes, as part of the curriculum, leadership class must be a mandatory and required part of the academic school day.

This is the future of education. Colleges are changing their admissions standards to place a greater emphasis on leadership.[18] Workforce development research consistently places leadership and leadership skills as the top 10 qualities employers are seeking in the graduates they hire.[19] In a world where leaders face increasingly complex challenges and circumstances that demand more from them and their teams than ever before, we *have to* equip students with these skills.

Evidence-based leader development in high school is ultimately going to be a way to prepare young women—and all students—to thrive in an uncertain and changing world.

In the words of Rebecca, a 14-year-old student at St. Ursula Academy, when asked to describe The Leadership Course™ to her peers: "Leadership class is the greatest opportunity you'll ever get in your life."

Biography

Julie Carrier, Founder of The Leadership Development Institute for Young Women, is an expert in leadership development for young women and girls and is recognized as the #1 Coach for Young Women. A former Senior Management Consultant in leadership training and development for the Pentagon, Julie is leading a movement to bring evidence-based leadership coaching and development—normally reserved for senior executives—to impact girls in high schools. In 2022, she was named to the Thinkers50 Radar list of up-and-coming thinkers whose ideas are making a positive difference in the world.

Notes

1. Thinkers50. "Identifying, Ranking, and Sharing Management Ideas," Thinkers50 About Us, September 22, 2022. https://thinkers50.com/.
2. Amy C. Edmondson, *Teaming: How Organizations Learn, Innovate, and Compete in the Knowledge Economy* (San Francisco: Jossey-Bass, 2013).
3. Carol S. Dweck, *Mindset: The New Psychology of Success* (New York: Ballantine Books, 2016).
4. The Leadership Development Institute for Young Women, "The Leadership Program: Outcomes," LDIYW, November 10, 2021. http://www.ldiyw.com/.
5. Susan Elaine Murphy and Stefanie K. Johnson, "The Benefits of a Long-Lens Approach to Leader Development: Understanding the Seeds of Leadership," *The Leadership Quarterly*, 22(3) (2011): 459–470. https://doi.org/10.1016/j.leaqua.2011.04.004.
6. David V. Day, "Integrative Perspectives on Longitudinal Investigations of Leader Development: From Childhood through Adulthood," *The Leadership Quarterly*, 22(3) (2011): 561–571. https://doi.org/10.1016/j.leaqua.2011.04.012; Adele Eskeles Gottfried, Allen W. Gottfried, Rebecca J. Reichard, Diana Wright Guerin, Pamella H. Oliver, and Ronald E. Riggio, "Motivational Roots of Leadership: A Longitudinal Study from Childhood through Adulthood," *The Leadership Quarterly*, 22(3) (2011): 510–519. https://doi.org/10.1016/j.leaqua.2011.04.008; Zhengguang Liu, Shruthi Venkatesh, Susan Elaine Murphy, and Ronald E. Riggio, "Leader Development across the Lifespan: A Dynamic Experiences-Grounded Approach," *The Leadership Quarterly*, 32(5) (October 2021). https://doi.org/10.1016/j.leaqua.2020.101382.

7. Thomas A. Kolditz, Libby Gill, and Ryan P. Brown, *Leadership Reckoning: Can Higher Education Develop the Leaders We Need?* (Oklahoma City, OK: Monocle Press, 2021).

8. Robert G. Lord and Rosalie J. Hall, "Identity, Deep Structure and the Development of Leadership Skill," *The Leadership Quarterly*, 16(4) (August 2005): 591–615. https://doi.org/10.1016/j.leaqua.2005.06.003.

9. Ryan P. Brown and Lebena Varghese, "Holding Higher Education to Account: Measuring What Matters in the Development of Students as Leaders," *Journal of Character and Leadership Development*, 6(2) (2019): 33–48.

10. M.A. Hoyt and C.L. Kennedy, "Leadership and Adolescent Girls: A Qualitative Study of Leadership Development," *American Journal of Community Psychology*, 42(3–4) (2008): 203–219. https://doi.org/10.1007/s10464-008-9206-8.

11. Kerstin Konrad, Christine Firk, and Peter J. Uhlhaas, "Brain Development during Adolescence," *Deutsches Ärzteblatt International*, 110(25) (June 21, 2013): 425–431. https://doi.org/10.3238/arztebl.2013.0425.

12. Chiye Aoki, Russell D. Romeo, and Sheryl S. Smith, "Adolescence as a Critical Period for Developmental Plasticity," *Brain Research*, 1654 (2017): 85–86. https://doi.org/10.1016/j.brainres.2016.11.026.

13. Brown, and Varghese, "Holding Higher Education to Account," op. cit.

14. Ibid.

15. Kolditz et al., *Leadership Reckoning*, op. cit.

16. Geoffrey L. Cohen and David K. Sherman, "The Psychology of Change: Self-Affirmation and Social Psychological Intervention," *Annual Review of Psychology*, 65(1) (2014): 333–371. https://doi.org/10.1146/annurev-psych-010213-115137.

17. Nathan Eva, Helen De Cieri, Susan Elaine Murphy, and Kevin B. Lowe, "Leader Development for Adolescent Girls: State of the Field and a Framework for Moving Forward," *The Leadership Quarterly*, 32(1) (2021): 101457. https://doi.org/10.1016/j.leaqua.2020.101457.

18. Tara Isabella. Burton, "Why Are American Colleges Obsessed with 'Leadership'?" *The Atlantic*, January 22, 2014. https://www.theatlantic.com/education/archive/2014/01/why-are-american-colleges-obsessed-with-leadership/283253/.

19. National Association of Colleges and Employers, "Job Outlook 2016: The Attributes Employers Want to See on New College Graduates' Resumes," NACE (2016). https://www.naceweb.org/career-development/trends-and-predictions/job-outlook-2016-attributes-employers-want-to-see-on-new-college-graduates-resumes/.

19

Servant Leadership, Cooperative Advantage, and Social Sustainability

Leon C. Prieto and Simone T.A. Phipps

Uncertain times require bold steps to face grand challenges. The list of challenges is long and seems to be growing longer every day: economic inequalities, climate change, the loss of biodiversity, and violations of human rights within global supply chains, to name but a few. The urgency of these issues is proof that things must change immediately because time is no longer a luxury we can afford. What is required now is a radically different philosophy of management; one that places cooperation at the center, and authentically values social sustainability.

This approach is not new. In fact, in Durham, North Carolina, during the Golden Age of Black Business, Charles Clinton Spaulding[1] led the North Carolina Mutual Life Insurance Company in a way that engendered community well-being from a systemic perspective. Through his enlightened leadership, Spaulding helped his company obtain a *cooperative advantage*; an approach rooted in African humanism.

Cooperative advantage refers to the benefits that an organization possesses and accrues due to its people-centered approach to engendering a spirit of care and community, meaningful dialogue, and consensus building for the benefit of employees, customers, community, and the entire value chain.[2] This definition stems from Abdul Bangura's conceptualization of Ubuntu, a South African philosophy (specifically Nguni Bantu), meaning "I am because we are."[3]

Organizations should strive not only to be profitable but also to ensure the well-being of everyone within their entire value chain. This means going further than thinking about visible stakeholders and putting measures in place to ensure that "invisible" workers in the Global South who are part of the global supply chain, work in safe conditions and receive a living wage. It means ensuring that the actions of the firm in no way harm any communities, including racialized ones. This requires leaders to think about ways to reduce negative externalities or the costs incurred by a company's operations during the process of developing products or services, where those costs have a spillover effect, such as harmful carbon emissions, and labor atrocities within the company's global supply chain. We need servant leaders who are committed to systemic change within organizations and who are equipped to lead us during these uncertain times.

The Role of Servant Leadership

According to Liden et al., there are seven dimensions of servant leadership:

1. emotional healing
2. creating value for the community
3. conceptual skills
4. empowering
5. helping subordinates grow and succeed
6. putting subordinates first
7. behaving ethically.[4]

Emotional healing is an important component of servant leadership, and organizational leaders who genuinely care about their employees' and community's well-being are needed even more now to influence and inspire change during these challenging times. Employees and communities have faced a great deal of hardship during these past few years as a result of Covid-19, racial injustices, and cost of living increases. Leaders who can empathize with others and implement initiatives and policies to address crucial issues usually achieve the buy-in that is necessary for them to succeed at the helm.

These leaders must also be equipped to *create value for the community* instead of being seen as just extracting value from the various communities that are integral to their ecosystem. Authentic servant leaders help the communities surrounding the organization.[5] However, there have been unsettling examples through the years of companies contributing to problems facing racialized communities in the Global South (e.g., water scarcity, poverty, child labor, etc.).

It is essential that organizations become better global citizens who respect our shared humanity. Thankfully, there have also been positive examples. For example, on September 14, 2022, it was reported that Yves Chouinard, the founder of the outdoor apparel brand Patagonia gave away his company to a trust that will use its profits to fight the climate change crisis.[6] This was a remarkable display of servant leadership that may spark further discussions and debates on stakeholder capitalism at a time when many people are concerned about the state of the planet.

Conceptual skills are important for servant leaders to help them understand their organization's goals, especially given the complexities that are facing today's workplace. The ability to see the big picture as it relates to corporate strategy while engendering a positive organizational culture that values teamwork is necessary for firms to tackle the issues related to sustainability. The *empowering* dimension of servant leadership involves the degree to which the leader entrusts the followers with responsibility, autonomy, and decision-making influence.

Considering the challenges that organizations are facing due to the so-called "great resignation," it is imperative that leaders drill down and determine the factors that lead to this challenge via a needs assessment. Organizational leaders must consider what employees need for their well-being, intentionally listen to them when they voice their needs, and work together with employees to reach an agreement. For employees to stop quitting their jobs in droves, they must feel heard and valued, and giving workers more flexibility, autonomy, and a better work-life balance may help, especially during these uncertain times.

Helping subordinates grow and succeed should be seen as a key ingredient in building any organization, but unfortunately, this is not always the case due to workplace incivility, inequity, lack of diversity and inclusivity, and other uncaring behaviors that are sometimes rife in organizations, potentially leading to burnout and psychological distress.[7]

Servant leaders help followers reach their full potential,[8] and may engender an organizational climate where employees thrive because all are afforded opportunities to benefit from desired employment decisions. In addition, servant leaders tend to *put subordinates first* because they prioritize meeting the needs of followers before tending to their own needs.[9]

For example, Tricia Griffith, President, and CEO of Progressive Corporation, stated that:

> CEOs work to generate profits and return value to shareholders, but the best-run companies do more. They put the customer first and invest in their employees and communities. In the end, it's the most promising way to build long-term value.[10]

Behaving ethically is another key component of servant leadership. Attributes such as being honest, trustworthy, and serving as a model of integrity are important to becoming effective servant leaders.[11] Hollywood portrayals of CEOs behaving badly seem to be the norm, but it is necessary for people to know that for every Logan Roy (fictional CEO on the hit series, *Succession*), there are examples from history and in contemporary times to follow, who proved that you can simultaneously lead effectively and compassionately.

Striving for a Cooperative Advantage

Servant leadership and cooperative advantage go hand in hand. A *spirit of care and community* is a core element of gaining a cooperative advantage and is reflective of servant leaders considering others and tending to their needs. Practiced in a business context, cooperative advantage addresses the kinds of values that embrace the well-being of the entire value chain.

One approach to gaining cooperative advantage is for corporate boards to hire CEOs with a well-documented commitment to community development and sustainability. Ideally, these individuals will have genuine interest and experience in fighting against social injustices, with consistent records of passion for and dedication to solving big problems.[12]

These types of individuals are well poised to understand the fierce urgency of now during these difficult times, especially as it relates to the multitude of grand challenges we are currently facing. Authentic servant leaders serving in leadership roles within our organizations are a key step to helping corporations align their mission to become better organizations; ones that value sustainable innovation and are more focused on making intentional modifications to a firm's products, services, and processes to generate long-term economic, social, and environmental benefits.[13]

Dialogue is another necessary component of cooperative advantage. Our shared humanity is being threatened by the grand challenges we are all facing, and there is an immediate need to foster bold and frank conversations throughout the organization to find solutions. To achieve a cooperative advantage, servant leaders should play a role in promoting dialogue to develop a culture that embraces learning from others, and to find solutions to the various problems facing the firm.[14]

Some of the novel ideas that are needed for corporations to become more focused on sustainability can be found right among the employees. For example, in the recent past, Xerox solicited ideas from their employees on how they could be more sustainable and efficient, and it resulted in them saving $10.2 million and eliminating 2.6 million pounds of waste.[15] Thus, they positively impacted both the organization and society.

Consensus-building is also instrumental in gaining a cooperative advantage. The facilitation of employees' voice as well as input from other crucial stakeholders (e.g., community members, workers in global supply chains, etc.) to aid in consensus-building influence increased cooperation, improved decision-making, and higher performance.[16]

For example, Shawn Askinosie, CEO of Askinosie Chocolate, forms robust relationships with cocoa farmers in Tanzania, the Philippines, and Ecuador, and they collectively work together to devise ways to mitigate risk and improve quality. Unlike larger chocolate companies with a questionable history of exploiting farmers within their global supply chain, Askinosie has developed a reputation as a servant leader who pays the farmers he works with above the fair trade market price for cocoa beans, and shares the profits with them.[17] He has demonstrated a commitment to striving for a cooperative advantage by genuinely caring for the farmers' well-being, authentically engaging in dialogue with them, and sincerely working together with them as partners to build consensus, resulting in mutual benefit for both parties.

Achieving Social Sustainability in Uncertain Times

In these challenging times, we need servant leaders who are focused on social sustainability. We need to reimagine management and adopt a philosophy of management that places cooperation at the center, instead of one that is powered by self-interest and unbridled capitalism. We need a greater focus on social sustainability. This means placing a greater emphasis on reducing economic injustices and human rights violations within global supply chains, as well as environmental challenges such as the climate crisis.

As long ago as 1937, Charles Clinton Spaulding said: "There must be social service in business. There has never been a time when my associates have not promoted the best interests of the community." His words are prescient and more relevant than ever. Corporations, especially those with a large international reach, must hold themselves accountable for prior social ills that they have contributed to, and must become more intentional in reducing harm to the global community in this age of ambiguity. Indeed, emphasis on achieving a cooperative advantage is necessary to embrace servant leadership, and pay as much attention to people and planet, as we do to profit.

Biographies

Leon C. Prieto is Professor of Management in the College of Business at Clayton State University, Georgia.

Simone T.A. Phipps is Professor of Management in the School of Business at Middle Georgia State University. They are Research Fellows at the University of Cambridge Judge Business School, and the authors of "African American Management History: Insights on Gaining a Cooperative Advantage," and "Cooperative Advantage: Rethinking the Company's Purpose," *Sloan Management Review*. In 2021, they were named to the Thinkers50 Radar list of up-and-coming thinkers whose ideas could make a positive difference in the world, and are the recipients of the Breakthrough Idea Award.

Notes

1. Charles Clinton Spaulding, "Business in Negro Durham," *Southern Workman*, (December, 1937): 1–5. Charles Clinton Spaulding was inducted into the Thinkers50 Hall of Fame in 2021.
2. Leon C. Prieto and Simone T.A. Phipps, "Reconfigure Your Board to Boost Cooperative Advantage," *MIT Sloan Management Review* (2021). https://sloanreview.mit.edu/article/reconfigure-your-board-to-boost-cooperative-advantage/.
3. A.K. Bangura, "Ubuntugogy: An African Educational Paradigm That Transcends Pedagogy, Andragogy, Ergonagy and Heutagogy," *Journal of Third World Studies*, 22(2) (2005): 13–54.
4. R.C. Liden, S.J. Wayne, H. Zhao, and D. Henderson, "Servant Leadership: Development of a Multidimensional Measure and Multi-Level Assessment," *Leadership Quarterly*, 19(2) (2008): 161–177.
5. Ibid.
6. Reuters, "Patagonia Founder Gives Away Company to Help Fight Climate Crisis." (September 16, 2022). https://www.reuters.com/business/retail-consumer/patagonia-founder-gives-away-company-help-fight-climate-crisis-2022-09-14/.
7. C.L. Porath, T. Foulk, and A. Erez, "How Incivility Hijacks Performance: It Robs Cognitive Resources, Increases Dysfunctional Behavior, and

Infects Team Dynamics and Functioning," *Organizational Dynamics*, 44(4) (2015): 258–265.

8. Liden et al., "Servant Leadership." op. cit.

9. Ibid.

10. Business Roundtable Redefines (August 19, 2019). https://www.business-roundtable.org/business-roundtable-redefines-the-purpose-of-a-corporation-to-promote-an-economy-that-serves-all-americans.

11. Liden et al., "Servant Leadership," op. cit.

12. Prieto and Phipps, "Reconfigure Your Board," op. cit.

13. R. Adams, S. Jeanrenaud, J. Bessant, P. Overy, and D. Denyer, "Innovating for Sustainability. A Systematic Review of the Body of Knowledge," Network for Business Sustainability (2012). https://nbs.net/wp-content/uploads/2022/01/NBS-Systematic-Review-Innovation1.pdf.

14. Leon C. Prieto, and Simone T.A. Phipps, *African American Management History: Insights On Gaining a Cooperative Advantage* (Bingley: Emerald Publishing, 2019).

15. L. Kaye. "Xerox Employees' Green Ideas Save Company $10.2 Million." *The Guardian*, November 15, 2010. https://www.theguardian.com/sustainable-business/xerox-employees-green-ideas-save.

16. Prieto and Phipps, *African American Management History*, op. cit.

17. S. Adams, "Second Acts: Why Shawn Askinosie Dumped His Law Practice to Make Chocolate," *Forbes*, May 9, 2017. https://www.forbes.com/sites/forbestreptalks/2017/05/09/second-acts-why-shawn-askinosie-dumped-his-law-practice-to-make-chocolate/?sh=69e82ab11015.

20

Leaders Talk Less and Speak Last

Modupe Taylor-Pearce

Since the invasion of Ukraine started on February 24, 2022, the world has been plunged into an energy and fuel crisis, with growing uncertainty in the medium- to long-term economic growth prospects. Livelihoods are being destroyed across the world, as well as lives being lost in Ukraine. The effect of fuel price increases and supply chain interruptions are being felt throughout the world. In Africa, where there is little economic wiggle-room for most citizens, the resultant increases in food and commodities prices are pushing African people into starvation.

On March 9, 2022, Al-Jazeera reported that the Russian President, Vladimir Putin, was "surprised" by the resistance being put up by the Ukrainian armed forces and its people against the Russians. He had apparently believed that the Russian army would be viewed as liberators and the Ukrainian people would support a return to "Mother Russia." It turns out he was mistaken, as the Ukrainian people have embraced their identity and are resisting the better-armed Russian soldiers. How did he end up making such a miscalculation on a project that has now wrought so much havoc on so many?

On March 30, 2022, Reuters reported that President Putin was surrounded by "advisers who are afraid to tell him the truth." The military leaders did not inform him that their troops were not logistically or emotionally ready for such an offensive and that the people of the country they would be invading would resist the offensive.

In 2016, in The Gambia, President Yahya Jammeh blissfully anticipated yet another landslide victory in an election that he was confident he would win. After claiming that he would rule The Gambia for "a billion years," Jammeh lost the election to a relatively unknown challenger (Adama Barrow) after 22 years in power. Jammeh was so surprised that he initially accepted, then rejected the election results. His advisors had not shared with him their concerns that his popularity among the Gambian people was waning, or that the average age of the Gambian populace (19) was so low that the youth who had not known any other leader were yearning for change.

When leaders talk more than they listen, they make poor decisions based on insufficient and inaccurate information.

These two examples have one thing in common: both Putin and Jammeh seem to be suffering from some kind of delusion or misinformation. Chances are they may either be not listening well, or those around them are terrified of telling them the truth. Either way, there is a leadership gap somewhere. . .

The higher a leader goes or the larger the organization that the leader has to lead, the more complicated and complex the problems become. As the problems become more complex, the leader's ability to recognize and use their team's perspective and knowledge becomes more critical to solving problems and accelerating growth.

Have you ever attended a meeting in which you felt, after the meeting, that the meeting was a waste of time? Have you ever felt that a few emails could have been sent to the participants and it would have had the same effect or an even better outcome than a meeting? Even if you have a single decade of work under your belt, you probably can attest to this feeling.

One of the reasons why some leaders struggle to successfully lead large organizations is because they are too quick to talk, and they talk too much. Let me illustrate with an example.

A friend of mine (fictional name "Abdul") who once served as a chief of staff to the president of an African country, experienced this when he attended his first few cabinet meetings with the President. His Excellency the President would introduce a problem that the country was facing and then he would proffer an opinion on what was happening and what should be done about it. Then he asked the Cabinet for their thoughts. The Cabinet Ministers, one by one, would almost trip over each other to register their effusive support for the President's opinion. After watching this for a few cabinet meetings, Abdul asked His Excellency to change his strategy. He said: "Sir, you will probably get better ideas if you don't share yours first." The next cabinet meeting, the President presented a problem (the country was never short of problems) and then asked for suggestions. There was silence in the room as everyone looked at the President to wait for him to share his opinion.

After what felt like five hours of silence but was only five minutes, the President finally broke it by proffering his opinion. This was predictably followed by a cacophony of "I concur with His Excellency" comments as the relieved Ministers enthusiastically registered their admiration for the brilliance of their leader. Abdul struggled to maintain his composure as he inwardly chafed with frustration. After the meeting, Abdul re-approached His Excellency and convinced him to be patient and wait for answers from his team.

The President reluctantly agreed and the next cabinet meeting, when there was a problem to discuss, he asked for suggestions and stayed quiet. The silence again felt like five hours before one brave Minister offered a suggestion. Everyone watched His Excellency to see if he would give an indication of what he thought about the idea. When he did not say anything, one by one, other Ministers offered opinions, some differing from each other. The President spoke last, summarizing what he had heard and offering his own opinion, which, he later shared with Abdul, had changed from what it was at the start of the meeting, based on what he had heard from the Ministers. In a meeting of decision-makers whose decisions affect millions of people, the President gained the perspective of a few more minds to make a better decision that positively impacted his people.

Why is it so important that leaders talk less and speak last? There are several reasons why it is important that, as a leader, you speak last or offer your opinion last. Here are three of them:

1. **What you don't know about the issue is greater than what you do know:** According to a 1989 study by Sydney Yoshida, called "The Iceberg of Ignorance," the leader of an organization is typically only aware of 4% of the problems facing the organization. By contrast, the frontline workers are typically aware of 100% of the issues facing the organization. This means that as the leader you should be continually aware that you are the least informed person in the room about the issues facing your organization and therefore should be the keenest to listen and learn from those who are more informed than you. If you make decisions when you are less informed, you are likely to make sub-optimal decisions.

2. **Regardless of what you think, it is difficult for your subordinates to disagree with you:** After you have spoken, it is difficult for any of your teammates to say anything contrary to your opinion. This is especially true in high power-distance cultures like we have in Africa, where it is considered culturally inappropriate to call one's elders or boss by their first name, or to look them straight in the eye (viewed as challenging authority) or to disagree with them. Even if you ask them for contrary opinions, as long as you have already given yours, they will be hesitant to offer theirs if theirs is contrary to yours. Therefore, it is critical that you do not offer your opinion on the matter until you have heard the opinions of all of the people in the room.

3. **Your team will be more vested in the implementation of the solution if they believe they contributed to it:** One of the common ways that our minds play tricks on us is to think that just because we have identified a solution, voilà!, the problem is solved. Even though we know this is not true, our brains continually try to convince us that it is. The identification of a solution is but the start of solving the problem. The solution has to be implemented and, invariably, implementation will encounter obstacles which have to be navigated by the implementers. As the leader, you are

hardly ever the implementer. If the implementer did not have input to the solution, then the likelihood of the implementer being willing to push through the obstacles is low, and the solution, even though appropriate, may be poorly implemented, yielding undesirable results.

Why is it so difficult for leaders to talk less and speak last? The reasons for this can vary based on the individual leader and their personalities and proclivities. I will share three of the most common reasons why leaders, especially African leaders, find it so difficult to speak last. As you read these, do a personal inventory of yourself to assess which of these characteristics you are most susceptible to:

1. **Hubris:** We like to show we are the smartest in the room. This may be one of the most dangerous and insidious traps of leadership. Hubris is pride gone amok, and before you say "Oh, it can never happen to me," let me assure you that if you are a leader, you are in a constant battle against hubris. The temptation to believe that because we are the leader/boss then we must be the smartest in the room is real, and it is dangerous. If you are the most intelligent person in the room, please do your organization a favor and recruit some more intelligent people! You are not the leader because you are the most intelligent or the most well-informed person in the organization; you are the leader because of your ability to influence yourself and others within and outside the organization to invest their time, talents, and treasure toward the achievement of the vision of the organization. This skill of influencing requires much more than just IQ.

2. **Stress:** Talking makes people feel relaxed and comfortable. Leaders are no different. We enjoy talking, because it makes us feel good and we feel less stressed. In meetings, especially with our subordinates, we enjoy it even more because our subordinates listen attentively (or at least they pretend to!). We also receive affirming feedback from our subordinates in the form of assertive nodding or grunts of agreement or outright praise when we talk, and this makes us feel good, relaxed, and smart. Who would not want to do more of this when it produces such stress-reducing results?

3. **Busyness:** We think it is more efficient to speak first, then the meeting will be briefer. Time is a precious commodity for every leader, and we are often constrained to sort out issues and move on to the next meeting or issue. It is tempting to believe that the process of listening to the voices of everyone in the room is a waste of precious time. It is true that the meeting might be briefer if we talked more and spoke first, but it also means the meeting will be less effective. If all we want to do is disseminate information, why not just send an email or a recorded audio or video with our thoughts? It would certainly save everyone else's time! The value of the meeting is to pool together the opinions of the attendees and engage them in discussions to find a consensus. This is best done when honest, open dialogue is engendered, and to achieve it, the leader must resist the urge to offer their own opinion until everyone else in the room has offered theirs.

In Conclusion

I recognize that for some of us leaders, this habit of talking less and speaking last may be an uncomfortable habit to adopt. If you find yourself guilty of one of the three vices that I have described in this chapter, let me suggest to you: GET HELP! What kind of help? GET A COACH! I recently coached one of my colleagues who was in charge of a large project that required significant coordination of a number of departments and external stakeholders. She was struggling with one key aspect of the project that was not going according to plan and was scheduled to have an update meeting on the project that day.

She shared with me her opinion of what needs to be done about the problem, and I coached her to run the meeting in the same way that Abdul coached His Excellency on the cabinet meetings. She hesitantly agreed to try it and three hours later, called me excitedly to say that she was delighted at the volume of great ideas and the commitment that were generated at the meeting. She said: "It was so much easier than coming up with the ideas by myself!" Indeed, leadership is all about influence. To influence most effectively, learn to talk less, and speak last. The organization needs you to give your best.

Biography

Modupe Taylor-Pearce is a Sierra-Leonean scholar (West Point, Cornell, and Capella University) and practitioner of leadership, management, and organizational development. A passionate pan-African, he is dedicated to transforming Africa through good leadership. He is the founder and CEO of Breakfast Club Africa Leadership, a pan-African organization that has impacted over 2,000 African leaders with leadership coaching, and the curator of the Made in Africa Leadership Conference. In 2022, he was named to the Thinkers50 Radar list of up-and-coming thinkers whose ideas could make a positive difference in the world.

V

Talent Magnets

21

Deciding Whom to Promote

Beware of "DEIB Debt"

Gorick Ng

When writing my *Wall Street Journal* bestselling book, *The Unspoken Rules: Secrets to Starting Your Career Off Right*,[1] I had a chance to interview a fourth-year university student from the US who had just returned from an on-campus information session hosted by one of his dream employers.

"So, what did you think?" I asked the student.

"I've changed my mind," he replied.

My eyes widened. I thought even the least desirable employers could make themselves look good within a two-hour period, especially with free food and corporate swag. What happened?

"Because no one looked like me," the student continued. "This employer had specifically invited members of the Black Student Union to the information session. But not a single person who came to represent the company was Black."

Intrigued by this student's reactions and how commonly held a view he had, I surveyed 706 professionals across industries and job types. I asked a single question: "How much more or less likely are you to join a team or company if there is no one on the team who shares your identity?"

Survey respondents were told that identity could be expressed in myriad ways, whether through ethnicity, class, gender, disability, or any other attribute one might be able to discern from a photo, biography, or online profile.

The results were astounding: 40% of respondents said that they were either "less likely" or "much less likely" to join the team or company if no one on the team shared their identity (Figure 21.1). Only about 5% of respondents were "more likely" or "much more likely" to join the team or company if no one on the team shared their identity.

Why are so many people "less likely" or "much less likely" to join a company where they are the "only one"? In the words of one respondent, "Who's on the team signals what a company's culture might be like and what opportunities might be available to me."

Perception does not always equal reality. Just because a team looks a certain way doesn't mean it is run a certain way. But just as employers have their biases toward talent, so, too, do talent have their biases toward employers.

In the world of technology, one of the most dreaded issues is "technical debt"—the situation you end up in when your software

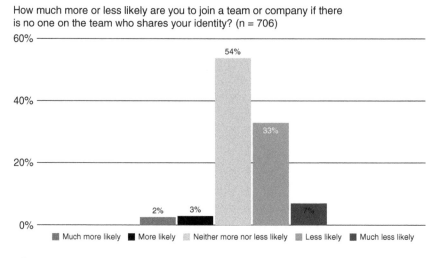

How much more or less likely are you to join a team or company if there is no one on the team who shares your identity? (n = 706)

Figure 21.1 Survey results.

development team prioritizes coding solutions that are quick but not necessarily scalable or sustainable. A quick fix here and quick fix there may not feel like a big deal in the moment—but then you look back and realize that you just built a house of cards. The cost of technical debt is high. Just open any piece of software that requires at least ten clicks to get anything done. The company knows the problem exists—it came from putting Band-Aids on Band-Aids on Band-Aids. It just can't get its thousands of employees and customers to stand still, tear the entire thing apart, and start anew.

If the challenge with building software is "technical debt," then the challenge with building teams is "DEIB debt" (where DEIB stands for "Diversity, Equity, Inclusion, and Belonging"). When filling a vacant position, it can be tempting to take the quick and easy path of looking left, looking right, and hiring your six closest friends. While the consequences of DEIB debt may not be immediately apparent, it is only a matter of time before the entire leadership team and board of directors looks the same and talks the same—and it is only a matter of time before prospective talent start asking themselves, hmm. . . this team is made up of all men; will I be taken seriously here if I am a woman?

Care about DEIB? Start now—and start with the next person you choose to "promote," whether in terms of who leads your company, represents your company, or speaks at your company.

Be Mindful of Who Leads Your Company

When building a team, put yourself in the shoes of a prospective job applicant you'd like to attract, a current employee you'd like to retain, and a potential customer you'd like to serve. Then, look at your company's team or leadership page and ask yourself: Can anyone relate to me here? If the answer is "yes," you're on the right track. If it's a "no," then it may be time to rethink whom you choose to promote and how you choose to showcase them.

When considering the "who" and the "how," consider both surface-level diversity and deeper-level diversity. Surface-level diversity is diversity from observable characteristics, such as gender, race, or visible disabilities. Deep-level diversity, on the other hand, is diversity from less-observable differences such as values, personality, and work preferences. When in doubt, ask your leaders to make their biographies and personal introductions more personal. Knowing that an individual is a "director" is helpful, but so is knowing that this individual came from a working-class background and had a challenging transition from STEM research to financial services.

Be Mindful of Who Represents Your Company

When sending team members to represent your company, whether at a career fair, in the media, or in a client meeting, put yourself once again in the shoes of your stakeholders. Then, ask yourself: What signals are we sending—and what signals do we want to be sending?

Signals can come not only from who is representing the company, but also from how they are representing the company. After attending a career fair, a college student once asked me, "Are expensive loafers part of the dress code at this company?" Another professional working in Asia for an American multinational corporation told me, "Everyone who spoke on the panel came from headquarters. Is there really a long-term career path for me here if I am not working based at the head office?"

Be mindful of the patterns you may be establishing. Two data points don't make a trend, but if there are only two representatives of your company in a room and both have some common characteristic, it can be tempting for onlookers to jump to conclusions about who can succeed—and not succeed—in your workplace. When in doubt, make the only pattern the pattern that all are welcome—and all can succeed.

Be Mindful of Who Speaks at Your Company

DEIB isn't just about sending a message to outsiders. It is just as much creating the desired culture for current employees. When running meetings, ask yourself: Is everyone I want to hear from given the space to speak—and rewarded for speaking? If the answer is "yes," you're on the right track. If it's a "no," then it may be time to rethink how you facilitate your meetings.

The first step is to avoid asking "What does everyone think?" Doing so not only rewards the most confident and fastest-reacting improvisers, but it also signals to everyone else that meetings will always get derailed by the usual voices. Call on the same people enough times and even the most motivated of the shy or introverted can start to wonder if their opinion matters. And sustain such a pattern enough times and you will soon find current employees whispering to newcomers, "This is just how things work around here."

If you are looking to conduct a vote, make it a blind vote. If you're looking to hear each person's opinion, have each person take turns. If you want each person to have an opinion, give attendees the prompt before the meeting. Give people the space to contribute before the weight of precedence is added to your company's DEIB debt—and no one you want to hear from ends up speaking.

In a world where everything is urgent and everything is due yesterday, thoughtfulness isn't always the behavior that gets rewarded. But, as the world begins to question the maxim of "move fast and break things" and in favor of a new way, may we also make talent choices that win both the fight and the war.

Biography

Gorick Ng is the *Wall Street Journal* bestselling author of *The Unspoken Rules: Secrets to Starting Your Career Off Right*. Named by Thinkers50 as one of the top 10 management books of 2022 and now used by organizations worldwide for talent development, it is a guide to help professionals, especially those from underrepresented backgrounds, take ownership of their careers. Gorick, a first-generation college student, is a graduate of Harvard College and Harvard Business School. In 2022, he was named to the Thinkers50 Radar list of up-and-coming thinkers whose ideas could make a positive difference in the world.

Note

1. Gorick Ng, *The Unspoken Rules: Secrets to Starting Your Career Off Right* (Boston: Harvard Business Review Press, 2021).

22

Justice at Work

David Liddle

The atmosphere in the team meeting was tense. Two colleagues, Sarah and Raj, had fundamentally different ideas about how the latest efficiency drive should be implemented. Both were digging their heels in and opposing camps had formed around them. Everyone was frustrated and debate was starting to become angry and disrespectful. Sarah accused Raj of bullying and undermining her, and straight after the meeting (which failed to reach any consensus), she headed to HR to launch a formal grievance.

This is an example of a scenario that is being played out every day in organizations all over the world. Employees fall out at work over how projects are managed, how resources are allocated, and how they relate to each other. Increasingly, they bring their strong views about social, political, and environmental issues into the workplace too.

Concepts of justice and fairness become the yardstick by which we measure the intervention (or lack thereof) of our managers and leaders. When issues remain unresolved, they can become damaging and dysfunctional; they burn hot. Stress and anxiety levels rise, teams become fractured, and the atmosphere quickly becomes toxic. Productivity takes a nosedive and employee engagement dips. Before too long, HR gets involved and the "rule" book gets pulled out. Time-consuming, adversarial, and often costly disciplinary and grievance procedures are invoked, and punitive performance management processes come into play.

These processes—which let's not forget have been designed for resolving workplace issues—are akin to pouring petrol on the flames. Worst case scenario, what often start out as quite simple misunderstandings or miscommunications rumble on for months, and eventually end up in front of a formal hearing or worse, in the courtroom. This paradox clearly can't be overlooked any longer.

There must be a better way?

Time for Change

How conflicts and disagreements are managed is a defining characteristic of the climate of teams. Team climate shapes the micro-cultures across an organization. Corporate culture is as an aggregation of team climate and micro-cultures. Therefore, the management of conflict and disagreement is a defining characteristic of the culture of our organizations.

At the heart of disagreement management and conflict resolution sits the concept of organizational justice. In other words, the concept of justice is a defining feature of our culture and conflict resolution and organizational justice should sit at the heart of any attempts to foster a positive workplace culture.

Research from the UK's Chartered Institute of Personnel and Development (CIPD) shows that conflict is a common occurrence at work, with over a third of employees experiencing some form of interpersonal conflict, either in the form of an isolated dispute or an ongoing difficult relationship, over a 12-month period. The associated costs are eye-watering, with estimates suggesting it costs UK businesses alone around £28.5 billion per year.

Yet very few organizations have any kind of strategy for tackling conflict. In fact, I would go so far as to say I have seen better strategies for ordering paperclips than I have for resolving the conflict that is tearing our organizations apart and getting in the way of innovation and productivity.

In an uncertain economic and political climate, where organizations are under pressure as never before, it's clear that something has to change. We simply cannot afford to carry on dealing with conflict in this damaging and ineffective way.

There are two key issues that need to be addressed before we can make progress:

1. Leaders and HR need to reframe the way they regard their relationship with employees. They need to develop a new social contract, which is fit for purpose in our agile, flexible, but extremely challenging modern-day environment.

2. Organizations need to move away from the damaging and divisive rules-based systems they use to manage the conflict, complaints, and concerns that inevitably arise as part of working life.

A New Social Contract

After years of working in organizations across the public and private sector, it has become clear to me that many organizations regard their employees more as a risk than an asset to the business. There appears to be an unspoken assumption that people, particularly at times of conflict or disagreement, are likely to cause harm to the business. The employer therefore becomes afraid of conflict (conflict-averse), and they begin to design it out and/or they create such a rigid and bureaucratic procedural framework that it makes it impossible for conflict to cause reputational or economic harm to the employer.

As the pandemic showed, however, most employees actively want to do a good job—and if treated justly and fairly, will willingly go the extra mile for their employer.

To develop and sustain a just, fair, inclusive, and high-performance culture, leaders need to embrace a cultural shift that we are seeing elsewhere in our society. They need to make it clear through their strategies and their policies that they realise that their employees are not a risk to the business—they *are* the business.

Instead of taking a reactive approach and focusing on mitigating people-related risks, they should be looking at how they can build people-centred, values-driven, fair, and just cultures, where people are able to be the very best versions of themselves. In these cultures, conflicts and disagreement are treated as potentially constructive and functional foundations within teams and managers, HR, unions, and others are equipped to manage disagreements constructively.

The organizations which are getting this right have begun to reframe their traditional rules-based systems and HR processes. They recognize that their formal policies and processes (disciplinary and grievance, bullying and harassment, performance management) are adversarial and retributive in nature. They understand that the old systems for managing people issues are centered around a right-wrong, win-lose mindset, with the needs of human beings conveniently pushed aside in favor of reducing the risk of an adverse outcome in any future litigation.

The organizations which are getting this right recognize that retributive justice creeps like a thief in the night, into the culture of their organizations and the climate of their teams. It steals the goodwill that has built up, makes off with the trust that has been earned and destroys the camaraderie that has been the glue that held their teams together. It makes their organizations, departments, and teams increasingly adversarial, hostile, and confrontational—destroying relationships and sowing the seeds of division.

Some leaders I work with go as far as to say that their current predilection for retributive justice erodes and undermines the very fabric of their organizations: trust, fairness, mutual respect, inclusion, and open dialogue. In other words, retributive justice breaks the fragile social contract in place in our organizations.

Introducing Transformative Justice

Transformative justice (TJ) is a new model of justice which is redefining the meaning of good work and the essence of good workplace cultures. By removing retributive justice (blame, shame, and punish), transformative justice underpins a person-centric and values-based workplace, and it offers a robust and compliant rule-based system where issues can be resolved quickly and effectively. Transformative justice is as powerful as it is impactful, and it delivers tangible results while maintaining that all-important need for regulatory and legal compliance.

This model of justice blends procedural justice (which is concerned with employee rights and the need for due process), natural justice (which is concerned with fairness and reasonableness) with restorative justice (which is concerned with reducing harm, promoting dialogue, and restoring relationships).

Transformative justice delivers a system of rules, behaviors, and processes which keeps people safe, builds trust, and promotes accountability. It is centered around dialogue, mediation, and facilitated conversations—with formal process only entering the equation when all other avenues have been exhausted.

It's an approach that protects relationships and generates constructive outcomes through meaningful dialogue. It is fair, empowering, inclusive, and tough. It holds people to account in a direct and powerful way—holding a mirror up and requiring us to ask ourselves some tough questions about the choices that we make and the impact of our actions on others.

When an organization adopts transformative justice, it often starts with the removal of their current discipline, grievance and performance management systems and replacing these with an overarching Resolution Framework.

In practice, this is what transformative justice looks like:

- **Really listening to what the other person is saying:** When we listen, it gives people a voice and demonstrates that we value them. It allows people to speak out, build awareness, and defuse tension.
- **Suspending judgment:** When we feel judged or evaluated, it makes us defensive (and we know that one of the best forms of defense is attack). By avoiding making judgments and by depersonalizing the situation, the risk of the attack/defend dynamic is reduced.
- **Putting ourselves in the other person's shoes:** The ability to be empathetic is a key feature of transformative justice. Stepping outside of our own reality and trying to understand what is going on for the other person can only ever be helpful.

- **Being compassionate:** Compassion is about being aware of the harm that our behaviors, systems, and processes can cause and reducing that harm by modifying them. Compassionate leaders create a psychologically safe space where employees can discuss their concerns and reflect on mistakes in a supportive and caring environment.

- **Seeking out areas of common ground:** This means stopping labeling other people and starting to engage with them as human beings. When we do this, we begin to understand that they too have needs, feelings, beliefs, motivations, hopes, dreams, fears, and aspirations. Often, when we start to engage with people at this level, it turns out their feelings and needs are very similar to our own.

As organizations move from retributive to transformative justice, they will find it delivers the following benefits:

- Workplace issues resolved closer to source, thereby reducing the time, the stress, and the money that may be required to fix them after a process of escalation.

- Greater levels of collaboration between key stakeholders. Collaboration builds higher-performing teams and creates synergies within our teams, divisions, and organizations.

- Greater levels of transparency and accountability. This ensures that issues can be highlighted and resolved earlier, and that people feel safer speaking up about concerns. It also means that errors and mistakes can be identified earlier, and the necessary changes made to resolve them and integrate the learning.

- Confident, competent, and courageous managers who can better predict, spot, resolve, and transform complex personal team and organizational challenges.

- Enhanced employee engagement, well-being, and inclusion, leading to better Employee Experience (EX) and Customer Experience (CX). This leads to great abilities to recruit and retain the top talent.

- Improved productivity with a more engaging and empowering system for measuring and rewarding performance, which drives motivation.
- A generally happier, healthier, and more harmonious workplace.

The use of transformative justice can also be applied to a wider industrial relations context. At a time when relationships between unions and management are becoming increasingly hostile and fractured, it is an approach that can be used to encourage collaboration and engender mutual support, respect, and trust. The principles of transformative justice encourage unions and employers to engage with each other in a predictive and proactive way. They enable each party to spot problems and resolve them before they escalate into collective disputes where positions become entrenched, and unions feel they have no option other than to withdraw labor.

The Role of HR

HR practitioners do, of course, have a key role to play in leading the charge to transformative justice. Many are supportive of this approach, and I am seeing some exciting progress on the ground with major airlines, banks, insurers, retailers, healthcare organizations, government bodies, and third sector organizations adopting transformative justice and models, such as my Resolution Framework.

One issue that often hampers progress, however, is a perception within the business that HR are the "organizational police," whose duty is to stand guard over the rules and processes. The ubiquitous "HR Business Partner" title, which still exists in many organizations, is part of the problem. It is a divisive and loaded term, which results in HR being perceived by many as the long arm of management. It erodes trust in HR, and it inhibits its ability to facilitate the fair, just, and dialogue-driven environment today's employees expect, and today's organizations need.

Senior leaders need to work alongside HR to shake off this mantle and to begin developing a truly independent and objective people-and-culture function where transformative justice is fully integrated into

HR's policies, processes, and procedures. It's about reimagining HR as the conduit between the culture of the organization and the climate employees experience on the ground. To achieve this aspiration, HR should focus on promoting a culture of trust, belonging, inclusion, dignity, and fairness—a transformational culture. The shift from transactional HR to a transformational people-and-culture function will help to attract and retain the top talent, the best investors, and the most valuable customers. That places HR as one of the most strategically important functions in the modern organization.

Courage and Fresh Thinking

As organizations strive to build back better following the global pandemic, and they prepare for the uncertain and complex times ahead, the cultural orthodoxies of yesterday will not be sufficient to resolve the challenges of tomorrow. A radical shift in the way our organizations think about justice is long overdue. Leaders need to ask themselves some hard questions about whether their organization's rules, procedures, and policies are reducing harm and really delivering a higher performing workplace—and how long they can afford to wait before adopting more compassionate, collaborative approaches that will equip them for future success.

Biography

David Liddle is the CEO of the TCM Group and author of *Transformational Culture* and *Managing Conflict*. In 2022, he was named to the Thinkers50 Radar list of up-and-coming thinkers whose ideas could make a positive difference in the world.

23

Personal Brand Building in a Creator Economy

Kai D. Wright

Leadership in uncertain times has shifted toward those with authenticity, relevance, and resonance. While CEOs may have powerful titles, creators from any walk of life can now quickly convert influence into big dividends while empowering communities. Whether you have a strong personal brand IRL (in real life) or in the metaverse, as the creator economy grows, more people are finding themselves uttering Jay Z's paradigm-shifting revelation, "I'm not a businessman, I'm a business, man." What does this shift mean for you as a leader, employee, entrepreneur, or beyond?

Follow the Feeling

Let's face it, brand building has evolved beyond the 2D art of a name, logo, and color combination; resilient brands are 3D forces fueled by strong communities united by a shared culture. And the difference between a fast-growing brand and one lost in the noise hangs on how you make others feel. So, whether an organization or person, there's an equal chance of building a resilient brand—regardless of whether you're an executive, entrepreneur, employee, entertainer, or anyone in between.

The new reality is that everyone has a brand, and your brand is more than just your reputation. Personal brands today are byproducts of many elements: what people think of you (i.e., reputation, purpose, vision, mission); assets you (co)create (e.g., logo, sonic identity, visual style); how you view the world (i.e., content, curation, and thought-leadership); what you make or provide to others (e.g., products and services); and how you behave (i.e., brand actions). And the strongest personal brands create clear value.

Globally, since 2010, "personal branding" has risen 200% as a search topic, while "branding" has remained flat.[1] It's not to say fewer companies have been created; in fact, there was modest growth. In the United States, for instance, in 2010, there were 28 million small businesses and about 4,000 publicly traded companies, while in 2021, there were 33 million small businesses and still 4,000 publicly traded companies. We are now in the days where someone with a strong personal brand can earn more than the CEO of an industry-leading multinational organization.[2]

In a creator-fueled economy, leadership has evolved. CEOs are no longer the most influential people in society. Now, over 50% of creators monetize their brand, and many are starting to earn millions while redefining the definition of a "work week." Is personal branding a trend here to stay or a fad that will fade, and how will it impact the future of work?

With more platforms launching viral, overnight sensations, it seems 15 minutes of fame is more economically worthwhile than ever. Gone are the days when a brand strategy cost a fortune to create, involved dozens of people to manage, or required 100-page brand guidelines to operate. We've learned three things about post-Covid society: (1) people are more resourceful and DIY; (2) authenticity creates brand stars that shine in any role or region; and (3) the pandemic has created new behaviors that keep any personal brand on the cusp of skyrocketing with one right talent, tweet, or TikTok.

In today's digitally connected multiverse, every person has to navigate a culture that can seem to change daily. What, then, are the macro factors to pay attention to when so much is in flux?

There are five factors causing a surge in personal brand management:

1. the rise of the creator economy;
2. the Great Resignation;
3. multiverse mania;
4. an ever-expanding media landscape;
5. accelerated digital transformation.

Whether an executive, employee, or entrepreneur, now is the time for vocal leadership. People yearn for inspiration, purpose, and expression as much as they seek professional pathways. Bye-bye corporate ladder. Leadership is now detached from titles and depends largely on your follower count, content ecosystem, and ability to catalyze a community emotionally.

Creating a future-proof personal brand that you can bank requires successfully navigating these five macro shifts.

1. The Rise of the Creator Economy

At the onset of the pandemic, everything slowed to a crawl or full stop—sports, film and TV productions, schools, travel, healthcare appointments, performances, and offices. And when supply chains began to crumble, and consumers had to re-evaluate how they spent their time (indoors), a new hero emerged: creators.

First appearing in the Merriam-Webster dictionary in 2016, the term "influencer" had long been used to describe celebrities and knowledge experts who endorsed and/or promoted products and services. As a result, "creators" have become a category unto themselves, first introduced at scale by YouTube in 2011 as they started to roll out monetization tools for influencers that specifically produced content.[3] Despite the headstart to the creator economy, by 2022, the fast-growing social platform TikTok had birthed new stars—Khaby Lame (150 million followers), Charli D'Amelio (145 million followers), Bella Poarch (90 million followers)—as YouTube, Instagram, and Facebook all faltered to keep pace.[4] Nowadays, the most-followed creators have platforms that surpass the reach of full US cable television penetration (76 million households), which peaked in 2010 at 105 million households. Having a large audience generally means influence, and we tend to think the most influential people in the world are CEOs.[5]

While CEOs were traditionally considered the most influential people in the world (pre-social selling era), creators now control the conversation. By 2015, only 39% of Fortune 500 CEOs were on at least one social media platform. By 2020, the number sat at 62%, with over 90% of those CEOs using LinkedIn as their primary social channel.[6] It's fair to say the average Fortune 500 CEO doesn't even have enough social followers to be considered a "micro-influencer" (i.e., 10,000+ followers). While CEOs flex their influence within a workforce or industry, creators move culture en masse. Leadership in uncertain times isn't about the power to tell people what to do but rather the relevance, resonance, and power influence to inspire people to mass action.

Case Study: MrBeast

Building a large community translates into major financial returns, rivaling the influence of organizations. MrBeast, the 20-something-year-old whose real name is Jimmy Donaldson, has amassed nearly 100 million subscribers on YouTube, placing him in the top five most-followed channels ahead of WWE (90 million followers).[7] In 2022, he turned down a rumored $1 billion offer for his channel—almost twice the sale price of media startup Axios to Cox ($525 million) and quadruple the market cap of once-media darling Buzzfeed ($235 million).[8] The news prompted Gary Vaynerchuk (a creator economy guru who teaches how to monetize digital presence) to estimate the MrBeast brand is worth over $10 billion—the same market cap as DocuSign, Hasbro, and Robinhood.[9] What's most interesting about the MrBeast brand is the speed of unlocking tangible economic value through product extensions. For instance, MrBeast Burger sold one million sandwiches in its initial two months. Creators have been so successful in turning their personal brands into products and services that the D'Amelio family, MrBeast, and investment firms are hunting for creator-led personal brands to help scale into products and services.[10]

2. The Great Resignation

In early 2021, Gallup found that over 60% of individuals were disengaged at work, with voluntary turnover at a 15-year high.[11] The high turnover was largely due to 30-45-year-olds (i.e., digitally savvy millennials and young Gen Xers).[12] By mid-2021, over 60% of workers were considering leaving their job; by mid-2022, McKinsey saw the number cool to 40% ready to depart.[13] Nonetheless, organizations have fought rising wages and recruitment costs as more people activated their personal brands to join the creator economy, add a side hustle to combat inflationary pressure on cost of living, or cut back to find pursuits that support passion and purpose.

The impact of the Great Resignation was evident on a platform where four people get hired every minute: LinkedIn.[14] To many—executives, managers, consultants, students, salespeople, entrepreneurs, financial experts, and others—LinkedIn is a professional calling card (i.e., a personal brand on a page). So, it may come as no surprise that in 2020, the average LinkedIn session was 6 minutes, but by 2022 the average session length had increased 25% to almost 8 minutes (along with higher page views).[15] The Great Resignation is pushing more people to evaluate their digital personas online, from social media to the metaverse.

3. Multiverse Mania

Brands must traverse the multiverse—from multi-player gaming (e.g., Grand Theft Auto, League of Legends) to virtual worlds (e.g., Roblox, Horizon). Globally, 70% of people have played a mobile game, nearly 50% of people have played a video game (e.g., Sony PlayStation, Nintendo Switch, Microsoft Xbox), and almost 40% of metaverse gamers are aged 10–20 years old (e.g., Minecraft, Fortnite).[16]

With eSports surging, the value of a brand built around a digital persona can be worth billions. In late 2022, one of the top three metaverses, Decentraland, had about 57,000 monthly active users (MAUs) and 6,300 monthly wearables sales (i.e., digital products).[17] By 2026, Gartner predicts at least 25% of people will spend an hour in the metaverse daily, with 30% of companies selling a product or service.[18] Research suggests that for someone who visits a store in the metaverse, there is a 70% purchase intent.[19] So creators with something to sell can strike gold with digital products, especially for designers. While big fashion brands like Nike, Dolce and Gabbana, and Gucci have already made $100+ million off digital goods, the metaverse offers budding or bold (fashion) designers, artists, and makers a chance to scale without the hurdle of real-world production and distribution.

But top creators aren't waiting to cash in on their digital personas. While the idea of influencers is not new, we are now in an age Bloomberg calls "cyber superstar."[20] Here's how we got here: social media sensations (e.g., the first person with one million "friends" on MySpace other than founder Tom Anderson was Tila Tequila in 2006), YouTube creators (e.g., Smosh was the first YouTuber with 10 million subscribers in 2013) and TikTok celebrities (e.g., Charli D'Amelio was the first person to amass 100 million followers in 2020). Personal brands are growing faster than ever, and the multiverse will create a set of new global leaders.

CEO of the world's largest tech company, Tim Cook of Apple, said he doesn't use the term "metaverse" because so few people understand what it is.[21] According to Ipsos, while 38% of people are familiar with the metaverse, only 16% can define it.[22] The metaverse today is what the internet was in its infancy: the Wild West of unclaimed territories (i.e., domains) that eventually may be a gold mine if you stake claims early. In other words, a speculator's paradise. Whether people understand what to do in the metaverse, or not, people are already managing multiple digital personas—social media, gaming, Web-connected devices, and beyond. Building a set of digital personas for the multiverse means your personal brand can possibly make more money (as you sleep) based on virtual goods than having a traditional 9-to-5 gig IRL (Table 23.1).

Clocking in more social media followers than most A-list celebrities, winning the multiverse with a personal brand can mean big business if you dominate a platform.[23]

Table 23.1 Leading multiverse personal brands in 2022

	Leading personal brand	**Multiverse brand value**
Minecraft	Dream (Clay)	50 million followers; each YouTube game-play video averages 20 million views
Twitch	Ninja (Richard Tyler Blevins)	18 million followers; earns over $40M in annual pay as one of the top-paid gamers
Roblox	Lyna (Evelyn "Lyna" Vallejos)	15 million followers; nets an estimated $50,000 monthly based on 10 million monthly views on YouTube game-play videos
Artificial Intelligence (AI)	Lil Miquela	5 million followers; brand valuation of $125 million based on modeling (e.g., Calvin Klein and Prada) and digital products (e.g., music on Spotify)

4. Ever-Expanding Media Landscape

In 2017, when Facebook was the #1 global app, a creative director revealed research that the average person scrolls through 300 feet of mobile content daily, which is the equivalent of walking up the Statue of Liberty with your thumb.[24] That year, over 300 hours of content were being uploaded to YouTube every minute. By 2022, over 500 hours of content were being uploaded to YouTube every minute—over 50% growth in video content alone in less than five years.[25] As we crave more filter options, leading personal brands help individuals navigate a growing sea of information, content, and choice, by adding an emotional human-factor. In essence, people want to feel connected to people.

While digital addiction increases and interventions such as Screen Time are helping track habits, the results are that more screens and more media choices lead to a waning attention span. Since the pandemic, the media landscape has become ever more expansive:

- More short-form video consumption (i.e., TikTok surged to beat Instagram in time spent on social apps, tying with YouTube at 45-minutes daily).
- More audio everywhere (i.e., podcasts and smart speakers became mainstream).
- More DIY learning (e.g., on-demand education hit 5× growth as schools and jobs shuttered).
- More skimming (i.e., newsletters and article summaries rose in popularity).
- More accessible formats (i.e., books, news articles, and mobile browsers became frequently available as an audio playback for easy listening options).
- More *à la carte* access (e.g., greater emphasis on selling single channels, chapters, episodes, and tracks rather than whole cable packages, books, seasons, or albums).
- More content in search results (i.e., social media content and/or images often outranked large, global websites in page results as timeliness trumped authoritativeness).
- More misinformation (i.e., most people didn't read links before re-sharing them on social media, prompting Twitter to change their UX in 2020 to intervene/nudge more caution when re-sharing trending links).

The proliferation of media also includes memes, gifs, and NFTs. During 2022, the buzziest news in art wasn't the largest art collection sale in history (i.e., Paul Allen's $1 billion lot at Christie's), the unveiling of the long-awaited Obama portraits, or the in-person return of Art Basel Miami. Rather, the biggest social uproar was AI-generated art that won first prize at the Colorado State Fair.[26] And as technology improves, personal brands will have to fend off deepfakes, from facial likeness to voice resemblance, setting up a battle over digital rights and enforcement as content grows faster than regulation.

5. Accelerated Digital Transformation

The pandemic reshuffled purchasing behavior—more niche, online, and social. Stuck at home, bread machines and free weights became out of stock across eCommerce platforms just as fast as masks and toilet paper. McKinsey revealed that during the initial 10 weeks of the pandemic (March–May 2020), eCommerce's 17 percentage point (pp) jump was equivalent to 10 years' worth of prior growth, which they dubbed "the quickening."[27] And who was there to cash in? Creators, makers, educators, and anyone with a personal brand that had a product or service to sell.

The pandemic created more ways to monetize personal brands—from higher shared ad revenue from video viewership or streams to DTC products on Etsy, Shopify, and Instagram Shops. In 2021, peer-to-peer eCommerce platform Etsy experienced 74% year-over-year growth to 7.5 million active sellers.[28] In 2019, Amazon and eBay rival Shopify had over one million merchants. In 2020, Black Friday and Cyber Monday sales on the platform nearly doubled year-over-year.[29] And by 2021, the Shopify seller base grew over 80% to over 1.7 million merchants.[30] Rolled out in mid-2020, Instagram Shops have amassed over 130 million active monthly users, roughly 10% of all platform users.[31] Finally, shopping became social and communal.

Despite how public their content consumption or shopping habits have become, consumers still want their data private. With Apple ending cookie tracking in 2021 and Google to follow by 2024, companies' relationship with their customers must transcend being data-driven. As expressed by cultural ethnographer Trisha Wang, access to "more" data doesn't lead to "more" insight or an improved ability to predict the future. COVID significantly increased the "noise" in data due to altered behaviors, misinformation, and the rise of new platforms (Table 23.2).

Table 23.2 Five factors giving rise to the era of personal brands

	The shift	Impact
1. Rise of the Creator Economy	More DIY tools and on-demand learning enables new ways to earn money P2P and DTC	You can become a paid personality, turning expertise into multiple scalable revenue streams
2. The Great Resignation	Constant evaluation of work-life prompts alternative pathways to sustainable living	You need to be discoverable and have a clear message to win SEO and attract brand opportunities
3. Multiverse mania	People now actively manage multiple digital personas across platforms, including metaverses	Your personal brand/s across platforms can build a combined core community of supporters
4. Media landscape expansion	More content consumed faster under waning attentiveness across mediums	Your personal brand must break through the noise by delivering clear (and immediate) value
5. Accelerated digital transformation	Widespread adoption of eCommerce, smart-home, social shopping, gamification, and private browsing	Your personal brand can create a multi-channel ecosystem and experience driven by behavior

Building a strong brand now requires evolving from a data dependency to high emotional attunement of communities—a shift that will crown new brand winners and losers.

The Future Economy

With over 33 million small businesses in the United States and a growing creator economy that encourages personal brand building, it may surprise some that according to the Bureau of Labor Statistics (BLS), the #1 projected industry in terms of wage growth between 2021 and 2030 will be promoters of events; agents; and (talent) managers.[32] So whether you are developing a personal brand for yourself, a client, or to benefit the organization you work for, now is the best time to invest in brand building. There's a whole generation not aspiring for executive titles, but rather building a personal brand they can monetize sustainably within a more relaxed lifestyle. And for CEOs and executives who want more authority, investing in a personal brand accelerates influence.

The brand-building playbook of the future will be personal, accounting for shifts during the pandemic that will have a lasting impact. Moving forward, people must rely less on data dependency to win audiences, less on media saturation through advertising to win attention, and less on fully controlling the customer or market to be resilient.

In the US, over 75% of people—including executives, professionals, and students—feel they don't have a strong personal brand. For many people, their personal brand has become what they do (i.e., their job), their identity (i.e., an American), or their geography (i.e., a Southerner). In the past 10 years, with the surges of societal issues, purpose/ESG, and "start with why" philosophies, many people are examining whether their current personal brand best represents their intersectionality, beliefs, or future vision.

Hip hop mogul Jay Z (Shawn Carter) shed light on the growing blurred lines between organizations and personal brands: "I'm not a businessman, I'm a business, man."

Strong brands are rooted in behaviors that empower communities and disrupt societal issues that inhibit lives. The behavior-based principles that drive product and service adoption, loyalty, and advocacy, are the same foundational principles of strong personal brands. You can ignite a personal brand that both returns economic value and activates empowerment, by starting to tap into your authentic self, crafting a clear message and POV on the world, mapping what your core community values most, and sparking cultural connections that keep you relevant to and resonating with communities. (Figure 23.1) Leadership in uncertain times requires making people better off, and anyone with an authentic personal brand can create radical value that matches the influence of CEOs.

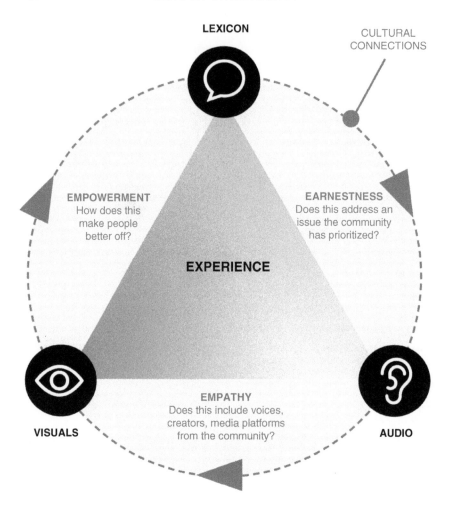

Figure 23.1 LAVEC model for brand building.

The LAVEC Model for Brand Building

The five components of resilient brands are: lexicon (e.g., branded vocabulary), audio (e.g., sonic signatures), visuals (e.g., conversation sparks), experience (e.g., normative behaviors), and cultural connections (LAVEC). To learn more about brand-building strategies and to access 50+ case studies of fast-growing brands, read the book *Follow the Feeling* and visit followthefeeling.com.[33]

Biography

Kai D. Wright is a strategic advisor to C-suite executives, founders, and celebrities. He advises on subjects, including brand building, digital, and DEI/culture. A frequent speaker at major conferences and Fortune 100 companies, Wright is an award-winning author (*Follow the Feeling: Brand Building in a Noisy World*), executive coach, and lecturer at Columbia University. He is a founding member of Ad Age's Diversity Council and host content series "System Overload: How Change Happens," which brings together top business strategists to demystify how to activate change management for DEI progress. In 2020, he was named to the Thinkers50 Radar list of up-and-coming thinkers whose ideas could make a positive difference in the world.

Notes

1. https://trends.google.com/trends/explore?date=all&geo=US&q=%2Fm%2F0b8xg4,%2Fg%2F121g0yc9.
2. https://advocacy.sba.gov/2021/08/31/advocacy-releases-2021-small-business-profiles-for-the-states/.
3. https://www.theatlantic.com/technology/archive/2019/05/how-creators-became-influencers/590725/.
4. https://www.dexerto.com/entertainment/top-20-most-followed-tiktok-accounts-loren-gray-charli-damelio-more-1326252/.
5. https://www.ibisworld.com/us/bed/number-of-cable-tv-subscriptions/4625/.
6. https://influentialexecutive.com/how-many-fortune-500-ceos-social-media-2020/.
7. https://www.nytimes.com/2022/09/13/business/media/mr-beast-night-capital.html.
8. https://www.axios.com/2022/08/08/axios-agrees-to-sell-to-cox-enterprises-for-525-million; https://finance.yahoo.com/quote/BZFD/.
9. https://youtu.be/GAyKb3jjBe4.
10. https://techcrunch.com/2022/03/04/damelio-family-launches-vc-fund-444-capital-to-invest-in-high-growth-startups/; https://www.theverge.com/2021/3/24/22348926/mrbeast-creator-investment-fund-creative-juice .

11. https://www.gallup.com/workplace/260564/heard-quit-rate-win-war-talent.aspx.

12. https://hbr.org/2021/09/who-is-driving-the-great-resignation.

13. https://www.mckinsey.com/capabilities/people-and-organizational-performance/our-insights/the-great-attrition-is-making-hiring-harder-are-you-searching-the-right-talent-pools.

14. https://business.linkedin.com/talent-solutions.

15. https://market.us/statistics/social-media/linkedin-corporation/.

16. https://www.luisazhou.com/blog/metaverse-statistics/.

17. https://cointelegraph.com/news/metaverse-platforms-refute-misinformation-about-daily-active-users.

18. https://www.gartner.com/en/newsroom/press-releases/2022-02-07-gartner-predicts-25-percent-of-people-will-spend-at-least-one-hour-per-day-in-the-metaverse-by-2026.

19. https://wwd.com/business-news/business-features/scalefast-metaverse-consumer-sentiment-1235045670/.

20. https://www.bloomberg.com/news/articles/2022-10-08/minecraft-star-dream-meets-his-screaming-fans-for-first-time.

21. https://www.cnbc.com/2022/10/03/apple-ceo-tim-cook-doesnt-like-metaverse-prefers-augmented-reality.html.

22. https://www.ipsos.com/en-us/news-polls/metaverse-opinion.

23. https://moneyinc.com/richest-twitch-streamers-of-2022/; https://www.twitchmetrics.net/channels/follower?game=Fortnite; https://www.bloomberg.com/news/articles/2022-10-08/minecraft-star-dream-meets-his-screaming-fans-for-first-time;https://outofthe925.com/famous-roblox-youtubers/; https://www.youtube.com/c/SrtaLynaV/videos; https://medium.com/illumination/meet-the-queen-of-the-metaverse-the-artificial-influencer-whos-now-worth-125-million-c6d0066a1a13.

24. https://market.us/statistics/social-media/linkedin-corporation/.

25. https://www.domo.com/data-never-sleeps#.

26. https://www.nytimes.com/2022/09/02/technology/ai-artificial-intelligence-artists.html.

27. https://www.mckinsey.com/capabilities/strategy-and-corporate-finance/our-insights/five-fifty-the-quickening.

28. https://www.businessofapps.com/data/etsy-statistics/.

29. https://investors.shopify.com/news-and-events/press-releases/news-details/2020/Shopify-Merchants-Break-Records-with-5.1-Billion-in-Worldwide-Sales-over-Black-FridayCyber-Monday-Weekend/default.aspx.

30. https://www.sec.gov/Archives/edgar/data/1594805/000159480 521000039/exhibit991pressreleaseq320.htm.

31. https://later.com/blog/how-instagram-changing-shopping/.

32. https://www.bls.gov/emp/tables/industries-fast-grow-employment.htm.

33. Adapted from Kai D. Wright, *Follow the Feeling: Brand Building in a Noisy World* (Hoboken, NJ: Wiley, 2019).

24

The Need for High Achievers in the Era of Uncertainty*

Ruth Gotian

The Great Reshuffle. Quiet Quitting. Whichever label you wish to put on it, employees are either walking out the door or not exhibiting the full array of their talent. They are likely doing their job, but not at their full potential. It is time to reimagine how we recruit, lead, and retain our most productive, effective, and innovative employees; the high achievers and their close cousins, the high potentials. They can become your organization's future, and you can earn a reputation as the leader with an eye for finding and building top talent. You can earn the reputation of a leader with the Midas touch.

Traditionally, leaders give most of the attention to our low performers, those who are not meeting predefined metrics. They get sent to courses and workshops to improve their skills. They have a supervisor who periodically checks in with them. Those who meet or exceed metrics don't get any of those opportunities.

---

* Information in this chapter is adapted from the book, *The Success Factor* by Ruth Gotian.

The high performers are watching from the sidelines. With great frustration, they are noticing where the company spends precious time and resources. The high performers recognize that the low performers receive a disproportionate percentage of the organization's investment. This imbalance may not be the intention, but it is the reality. Before long, your high performers will resign or quietly quit, meaning they will no longer be working to their full potential, but still collecting a paycheck. As a leader, at best, you will be left with the average employees and, at worst, with your low performers.

What if you gave the high achievers opportunities to learn, stretch, and grow? The high achiever's mind is always working, never shutting off. They continuously wonder what if, how, and why. They want to dive deeply into certain topics and learn new skills. They are very much aware that they have a void and are unaware of what they do not know. The good thing is that they are always willing to figure it out and seek to consume new knowledge.

Learning Development Plan

While they are likely having great conversations with people, listening to podcasts, and watching endless webinars, perhaps consider creating a learning development plan for the employees you'd like to see grow and advance within the organization. Ask them what they would like to learn or if they have any conferences in mind that they feel would be helpful to their learning and career. While getting another degree is certainly one option, and don't take it off the table if it is viable, taking targeted courses or workshops might be a better approach in certain situations.

If your high performer does not know what is available, ask them what they are curious about and suggest some courses, conferences, or workshops. In addition, encourage them to talk with someone with expertise in that topic, and take it a step forward by making an introduction.

Providing a learning allowance will allow employees to determine how to spend it to meet their learning goals. Serve as a sounding board so they can bounce ideas off you. They should see you as someone who opens doors for them not slams them shut. Having them learn new skills and support their innate desire to learn will pay dividends.

High achievers implement what they've learned immediately so the innovation will return to the workplace instantly. It is a fantastic way to bring new ideas into the organization without constantly hiring and onboarding new people. Just keep supporting the upskilling efforts of your top employees.

Stretch Assignments

The best learning and development happen right outside our comfort zone, so it is important to routinely stretch beyond our natural capabilities. As long as the challenges are appropriately supported and scaffolded, meaning the employee knows there is a safety net of people and resources they can turn to, stretch assignments are a great opportunity for the high achiever to learn new skills on the job and showcase their capabilities.

Situational Leadership

When they have taken the lead on a project, let them present it to the higher-ups. The exposure and recognition will help them take ownership of their work and will show that you, as a leader, are capable of situational leadership—the ability to give the spotlight to the person who knows most about a topic.

Room to Work

High achievers fear not trying more than they fear failing.[1] They love a challenge as it is a puzzle that needs solving. They never question *if* they can overcome a challenge. Instead, they focus on *how* to overcome the challenge. They wonder what strategy they have yet to consider.

As these productive employees work, doodle, and ideate, avoid hovering. Give them the space they need to figure things out. Micromanaging them or constantly checking in with them will cause them to break their concentration, and you will lose your credibility. What could be revolutionary will be littered with interruptions, second-guessing, and loss of confidence. It will not serve anyone well. Instead, give them the space they need to figure things out. Let them know you are there should questions or concerns arise. Be their safety net, not their choke hold. It may seem disorienting to you as a leader not to be aware of every step of a process, but you hired them because something you saw in them raised your eyebrows. You made them a job offer because you were impressed with their background and potential and were curious about what they could bring to the table. Now is the time to trust your instincts and realize you knew what you were doing when you hired them. It's time to make that dream a reality. Now let them show you what you dreamed was their capabilities that they could bring to the organization. Express interest and curiosity, but do not get under their skin.

Don't Disrupt the Flow State

This ambiguity might drive you crazy as a leader, but there are ways to still get the knowledge you seek without appearing as if you do not trust them. While a check-in meeting might seem like the right approach, what if this meeting is scheduled just as your top employee is in a state of flow?[2]

A state of flow is when you are in a deep concentration, at your most productive, and at your happiest. You are dealing with a mix of comfort by working on something you are familiar with, yet also appropriately challenged so that you get to think deeper and try new things. A flow state is what every high achiever hopes to achieve to optimize their productivity and creativity.

Imagine they had a scheduled meeting to give you an update when they were in a flow state. That would be incredibly frustrating. Instead, see how you can informally get the information you are seeking. Remember, you do not need details, just broad strokes of what they are working on, because you trust them. Is there a natural time of the day they take a break? Is the coffee room appropriate for a "How's your project going?" conversation? Perhaps. If you want more information, offer to take them to lunch. This way, they can eat and give you an update. Ask questions that show interest, such as, "What is the biggest challenge you are trying to overcome?" or "What surprised you?"

Inner Mobility

High achievers want to know that they have a future within the company, and that you, as a leader, can help achieve their next promotion. They do not want to be stuck in the same job, doing the same work just because their boss is stuck in their role or, worse, is not motivated to advance. Sit down with your high achiever and review their strengths and areas of potential growth. Be transparent about where you see them advancing in the organization. Offer a timeline. High achievers like goals, and having one to smash is something that will get them fired up.

Your top employees want to know that they have mobility within the company, with new challenges, goals, and opportunities available. Share what you have in mind for them, and coach them to achieve it.

Reward Your High Achievers

When your top employees are doing something well, be sure to recognize it. Do not glorify common expectations, such as arriving on time or keeping a neat workstation. That is belittling, and they will not take you seriously. But if they beat a deadline, came in below budget, or had a great idea, recognize them publicly for it. They want to know that you recognize their work.

As a leader, you know that not everyone who works together in a group carries the same level of output or weight. Be sure to differentiate your recognition of those pushing the group forward with their ideas or productivity. Do not recognize everyone in the same way, as that will highlight that you do not recognize the different values each person brings.

While high achievers want to be paid what they are worth, it is not necessarily their driving factor. They want to see that you, as the leader and the organization, value curiosity, innovation, and creativity. If, as a leader, you are showing that you value how it's always been done more than how it could be, or better yet, what it could become, you have lost your best employees. They want to see that you are always raising the bar for yourself and others as a leader.

Mentor Them

Having employees eager to do well means they sometimes get in their own way. They lack perspective and are in desperate need of guidance. Mentor them, and encourage others who should be on their mentoring team.[3] Guide them, cheer them on, and be their friend and confidante when they need one. Push them out of their comfort zone and shelter them from the toxic people and politics that plague every organization.

We are all like rubber bands, able to stretch beyond what we thought possible, as new opportunities emerge. The more you stretch, the less likely you will fall back into your old ways. The good part is that you will not want to. That is the mindset as you encourage your high achievers and give them the tools they need to succeed.

Helping your high achievers learn, stretch, and grow will serve as a great retention program and help in your recruitment. High achievers tend to associate with others like them. If you treat them appropriately, guide them, push them, and encourage them to excel and have upward mobility within the organization, they will tell their high-achieving friends about it. Before long, these others will want to join your organization, and your high-achieving employees, whom you have treated well, and they will become your biggest fans and recruiters. You will soon lead an organization of high achievers, pushing the bar of excellence, and be known as one of the best places to work. You have the potential to be an industry leader if you lead these overlooked employees in the right way. You have now realized that supporting high achievers is not just a good policy; it makes business sense too.

Biography

Ruth Gotian is the Chief Learning Officer and Assistant Professor of Education in Anesthesiology at Weill Cornell Medicine. She is the author of *The Success Factor: Developing the Mindset and Skillset for Peak Business Performance*. Her work regularly appears in *Forbes*, *Psychology Today*, *Nature*, *Scientific American*, *Academic Medicine*, and *Harvard Business Review*. In 2021, she was named to the Thinkers50 Radar list of up-and-coming thinkers whose ideas could make a positive difference in the world and received the Thinkers50 Distinguished Achievement Radar Award.

Notes

1. Ruth Gotian, *The Success Factor: Developing the Mindset and Skillset for Peak Business Performance* (New York : Kogan Page, 2022).
2. M. Csikszentmihalyi, *Flow: The Psychology of Optimal Experience* (New York: Harper & Row, 1990).
3. Ruth Gotian, "How to Develop a Mentoring Team," *Forbes*, July 6, 2020. https://www.forbes.com/sites/ruthgotian/2020/07/06/how-to-cultivate-a-mentoring-team-in-five-easy-steps/. accessed September 3, 2022.

VI

Relationships@Work

25

Curve Benders

Quality vs. Quantity of Strategic Relationships in the Future of Work

David Nour

The key characteristic of twenty-first-century business is instability. Companies can no longer be confident of their hold on customers, markets, or even their own employees. We can't predict which products, technologies, or even entire industries will take off, while others stagnate.

In this environment, we need to rethink professional relationships that lead to career development. The conventional wisdom emphasizes the power of weak ties: the advice is to connect with a lot of people, including many in different industries, areas of expertise, regions, or social circles. To get to the next level in your career—either a job offer or an introduction to someone with an opportunity—you need to cast a wide net: it's all about quantity over quality. You're likely to get a break not from your friends, this logic says, but from someone you barely know. Developed in the 1970s by the sociologist Mark Granovetter, this approach continues to be the common advice to people looking to advance in business.

Weak ties may have worked well in the late twentieth century, but they fall short in our uncertain today and tomorrow. I've coached dozens of ambitious executives over the past decade, and I've seen a different story—the benefits of investing in fewer yet dramatically more strategic relationships. Instead of appealing to a great many possible leads, my experience suggests you are better focusing your efforts on developing medium-to-strong ties with a far smaller group.

The Changing Landscape of Advance

What's changed? I see three key developments. The first is simply our declining attention span. We simply can't keep in mind the names of people we barely know, compared to how earlier generations did. Those powerful computers in our pockets are making it harder, not easier, for us to connect our broad network to possible opportunities. Weak ties are just too weak—to stay top of our mind, we need to deepen our relationships with fewer people.

That's especially the case because the nature of business opportunities has changed. In the twentieth century, most of the good jobs were at big organizations with well-defined hierarchies and markets, and people had clear areas of expertise. Now we have an amazingly diverse landscape of companies big and small, with organizational structures changing overnight and opportunities emerging out of nowhere. Instead of semi-permanent jobs, people are open to projects lasting months or years. Major areas of expertise now in demand didn't even exist a generation ago. Business is increasingly interdisciplinary. It depends on innovation, not execution or optimization; all the low-hanging fruit has been plucked.

It's also now much easier to find your own startup, to chase your dream as an entrepreneur, rather than accept a corporate position. We aren't trapped by whatever the universe offers—we can create our own future.

After all, most opportunities aren't straightforward jobs with obvious appeal—it's a possibility with a mix of variables to assess. Even for corporate positions, companies increasingly expect applicants to design the role and the strategy for the division or department. This is even more the case in uncertain and fast-changing times. And just as the job can't be reduced to a sentence, people can't either. Hence the power of strong ties, with people who know something about you and can do some advance thinking about your suitability for the lead.

Just think about Covid-19. Many people expected a global pandemic at some point, but not one that would last for years and transform workplace collaboration. When Nassim Taleb talked about black swans in 2007,[1] few people took him seriously, but then we got the Great Recession, and now Covid-19. Expect more disruptions to come at an increasing pace.

Third, those weak ties are much harder to make now than in the past. This was happening even before Covid-19 hit, but the pandemic has accelerated the shift. Corporate jobs used to afford lots of time for outside interests, hobbies, civic engagement, and industry functions. Whether for good or ill, ambitious people have less time for those activities. And now the pandemic drastically reduced the number of in-person events, not to mention time in the office. Serendipity used to provide a lot of weak ties with little effort on our part.

Post-pandemic, we're going to have fewer in-person gatherings, and we'll need them to be more intentional. Forget networking parties—now we need to be strategic in how we connect to people. We'll also need to learn to invest in relationships that are primarily digital—Zoom visit rather than coffee or lunch.

Business Relationships as a Strategic Assets

It may sound crass, but when ambitious people have fewer yet stronger ties, they need to think about those ties differently. And the most important relationships will be mentors. Not a corporate elder who can guide you up the hierarchy, but someone with a bit more experience or expertise who can help you make sense of your opportunities. A lead or job offer by itself, after all, isn't as valuable as it used to be— you need to assess whether it fits your skills, interests, passion, purpose, and vision.

The best mentors become what I refer to as curve benders, because they help you rise to the next level, often in unexpected ways. They'll accelerate your learning curve, growth, and adaptation. In conversation with them, you'll figure out what really drives you and where you want to commit your energy. Unlike transactional mentors who pass on information, along the way, especially as you rise into leaderships roles, you'll want to be curve benders to others, both to experience the role from that perspective and to learn from them. The older you get, as you've achieved success and now seek significance, you'll want to mentor even more.

After all, in our unstable world, any mentor you find is likely to be searching for information and opportunity as well. So be prepared to add value on your end as well. That's part of the investment, but together you and your mentor may devise opportunities neither of you could have imagined on your own. Just as new business opportunities emerge in unpredictable, non-linear ways, your greatest success might well come from implementing ideas immediately rather than perfecting them in a textbook linear process.

Just as venture capitalists and companies can't put money into every interesting possibility, you need to invest carefully in a limited number of deep relationships. Those are the strong ties that will push you forward in your personal, professional growth and ultimately, career. Chasing a lot of weak ties will leave you with shallow conversations. You'll be a well-connected dilettante who hears a lot of gossip but doesn't stand a chance in landing one of the big opportunities.

How to Invest in Relationships

There are seven main steps or principles for investing in strong, mutually valuable, and lasting business relationships:

1. Like all investors, you need to have a plan at the outset. You'll probably change the plan over time, but a plan gives you initial direction and enables to you to choose among a flood of potential connections and conversation topics. Try to visualize the problems or areas you'd like to work on, and at what level or kind of company.

2. We all have a limited amount of time to invest in relationships. Contrary to weak ties, I tell people to start with their existing relationships, the contacts they already know well. Focus on a few people you already enjoying engaging with and who have impressed you with their awareness of interesting areas. Remember to give as well as get; make those ties mutually advantageous. You must already have some ideas about the areas that interest you—try them out with one of those quality relationships. You'll only get smarter.

3. You should still seek out new relationships, both to diversify your reach but also because most opportunities cut across disciplines. The conventional wisdom has one thing right: we need to connect with people beyond our comfort zone. Look for people who fill in gaps in your access to key areas, developments, and firms. Consistently aim for quality, not quantity, and invest in the people who excite you. Back in 2013, an ambitious young man from Turkey sought an internship at my small firm in Atlanta. I could have passed, or when he arrived, treated him with only minimal attention. But instead, I gave him a chance, and I tried to learn from him while I and others taught him the business. Diversity matters now more than ever because opportunities aren't emerging in predictable ways.

4. Next, look for new people well placed in your areas of interest, and see if you can connect the dots to them from people you already know. Here's where those deep ties pay off: every introduction or referral is a recommendation. Don't ask for favors from people who still know you only a little.

5. Stick to the process. If you're truly ambitious about rising, you'll muster the conscientiousness to keep those relationships fresh and creative. Relationships rarely pay off at first; it's only as you get to know each other that you discover possibilities.

6. Think career lattice, not ladder. Ladders are narrow, unidirectional, and predictable. When you climb a lattice, you might come across unexpected barriers and go sideways for a while, but you're still progressing. Or maybe you're not even sure where you want to emerge at the top, so you'll want to range across for a while. Trying

different kinds of work helps keep you flexible and open-minded, not trapped in a specialty.

7. Believe in abundance and seek mastery. It's easy to think, "if I don't get a specific kind of job, I'll be a failure." The reality is that no one knows what the cool jobs (or projects) will be in the future. Instead of focusing on a job, focus on a problem or challenge, and work on addressing that problem. You might not proceed as you expect but throw away your stopwatch and get a compass. If you're going in a good direction, learning, and growing, then you're fine. Any problem worth solving is going to need a bunch of people, not just you, so welcome collaborators.

Strategic Relationships in Action

One executive I'm coaching epitomizes this change. She's an accomplished computer programmer who has worked only in technology, and she took an offer with her current company two years ago. The company made her a senior vice-president, but the CEO values her mainly for her tactical IT skills, and she's increasingly thinking broadly.

This is a increasingly common case of understandable but misaligned expectations. But if she followed weak ties logic, people would think of her only as an IT person. She might get flooded with offers, but not in the area she really wants.

I gave her the advice about strong ties, and she's been expanding her sights to discover her passion. Turns out she's most interested in marketing, based on some projects she's done with the CMO in the past. So, she's been investing in relationships with people in marketing. She's found people who can make her savvy in that area, while she teaches them about tech. In one-on-ones and small groups, they're discussing how marketing—now in a kind of crisis—can take full advantage of emerging technology.

I'm confident this targeted investment is going to pay off handsomely for her. With her relationships, she's developing the knowledge and skills to position herself for whatever opportunities emerge. I don't know where those opportunities will come, but I'm confident she'll have the smarts, and the advisors, to choose the best one for her.

It's time to get past our twentieth-century notions of personal growth and career management. Business today is too fluid and complex to rely on a shallow net of information leads. You'll get much better information, and insight, from a small yet deep portfolio of strategic relationships.

Biography

David Nour is a senior leadership advisor, and an executive coach based in Atlanta, Georgia. He is the best-selling author of *Curve Benders: How Strategic Relationships Can Power Your Non-Linear Growth in the Future of Work* (Wiley); *Co-Create* (St. Martin's Press), and *Relationship Economics* (third edition, Wiley). In 2021, he was named to the Thinkers50 Radar list of up-and-coming thinkers whose ideas could make a positive difference in the world.

Note

1. Nassim Taleb, *The Black Swan* (London: Penguin, 2007).

26

Navigating Ambivalence in Our Professional Relationships

Amy Gallo

How we get work done, especially in an age of extreme uncertainty, depends on the quality of our relationships. You can have the smartest strategy, the most talented people, top-notch systems, and processes, and you can still fail if the people behind the execution have strained interactions and don't get along. Put simply: our relationships with our colleagues—our bosses, leaders, peers, and direct reports—matter.

When those relationships are strong, they are a source of energy, support, growth, and productivity. But when they fracture, they cause us anguish, frustration, and stress; they undermine our ability to do our jobs. Research by Georgetown professor Christine Porath and her colleagues found that de-energizing relationships have a four to seven times greater impact on our well-being than energizing, positive relationships.[1]

Of course, not all of our work relationships fall neatly into categories of "positive" or "negative." There are those that we feel unsure or conflicted about. These "ambivalent relationships" are often just as problematic as the unambiguously negative ones.[2]

When I think about the people I've worked with throughout my career, many of those who stand out as challenging weren't actually difficult *all the time*. For instance, I had a colleague who I'll call Tara. We were never friends exactly, but we enjoyed chatting at the beginning of meetings and, at social events, she and I often talked about our young families. I found her funny, personable, and good at her job—most of the time.

When I got up the nerve to ask another coworker whether he also found her difficult to read at times, he perfectly articulated what I was experiencing: "You just never know which Tara you're going to get. 'Good Tara' is really nice and seems to have your back. But 'Bad Tara' is grumpy and focused on her career and has no qualms about throwing you under the bus."

When you work with someone with whom you have an unequivocally bad relationship, it's no walk in the park, but at least you know where you stand. When you work with someone like Tara, whether they're your boss, your peer, or a member of a team you manage, it can feel destabilizing. You might walk on eggshells around them, watch your back, and wonder: "Are they on my side? Or not?"

Some studies have shown that a good number of our relationships fall into this more nebulous category—as many as 50%.[3] They may be so prevalent because we're essentially stuck with our coworkers. It's rare that we get to choose the people we work with and, because of these enforced interactions, it's easy to feel ambivalent about them.

These connections with colleagues—those that aren't all good or bad—can take up a lot of space in our minds, causing us to question our talents, competence, and sanity. And research has shown that they're often worse for us, on a physiological level, than a purely negative relationship. Studies have connected them to higher blood pressure, lower resilience, poorer overall health, and stress.[4] They've also been shown to increase time spent ruminating and feelings of guilt or envy.[5]

Interestingly, they have upsides too. Sometimes they motivate us to work harder because of the productive competition and we're more likely to try seeing things from the other person's perspective as we struggle to understand them.[6] We may also put more time and energy into improving the relationship, whereas we might take a purely positive tie for granted.

So how can you navigate these relationships to manage the downsides and amplify the upsides?

Accept Ambivalence as Normal

Leaders are often encouraged to be decisive. And when things are uncertain in your company, your industry, or the world, ambivalence can be unsettling. We want things to be clear. There's a concept in social psychology called "cognitive consistency" that argues that we prefer for our thoughts, beliefs, and opinions to be congruent, and when they're not, we feel discomfort. But it's normal to feel two ways about something; for example, it's possible to both admire and loathe a colleague. And it can be a leadership advantage to hold conflicting opinions and emotions at the same time. As F. Scott Fitzgerald wrote, "The test of a first-rate intelligence is the ability to hold two opposed ideas in the mind at the same time, and still retain the ability to function."[7] Accepting that we feel ambivalently about the people we work with can help us make better choices about how to interact with them.

Similarly, we have to accept *their* inconsistent behavior. Instead of trying to resolve it (*there shouldn't be two versions of Tara!*), tell yourself that everyone behaves inconsistently at times and it's not your job to force them to change.

Control "the Controllable"

The reality is that few people alter their behavior because someone else wants them to. They do it if and when *they* want to.

I've been in many situations where I thought, "If I can just explain to the other person how their inconsistency is impacting me, surely they'll understand." But as Wharton professor Adam Grant says, sharing our logic doesn't always work. He writes: "I no longer believe it's my place to change anyone's mind. All I can do is try to understand their thinking and ask if they're open to some rethinking. The rest is up to them."[8]

If getting along with your colleague is entirely dependent on your ability to convince them to become a different person, you're taking a big risk. They may not have the capacity to change, or they might not want to. The only control you really have is over yourself—your thoughts, feelings, and reactions.

I have a Post-it note I keep by my desk with a mantra borrowed from my friend Katherine's daughter's school. At the beginning of each day, they all recite this together:

My body is calm.

My heart is kind.

I am the boss of my brain and my mind.

On days when I'm struggling with a nasty email or gearing up for a difficult conversation, I'll read it out loud to myself. It's a good reminder that even when I'm overwhelmed, I still have agency over what matters.

Observe and Analyze

When we're interacting with someone who pushes our buttons, to make sense of what's happening, our brains form a narrative that gives the person's actions meaning. We quickly tell ourselves a story about what's occurring, why it's occurring, and what will happen next. And these stories—laden with emotions and critiques—feel truthful to us even when they're based on our brain's sense-making attempts rather than on facts.

Try to challenge those stories and observe what's really happening with your colleague. Take note of when they act more positively toward you (is it after you've paid them a compliment? When you're talking about a specific project? In front of others?) and when they are more competitive or negative with you (is it when you're alone? On email? When they're under pressure to deliver?). Attempt to do this without judging their behavior but just observing it. The hope is that you can start to predict what sort of reaction you're going to get so you aren't blindsided by their more negative actions.

Interrogate Your Biases

Our interpretation of a colleague's behavior is often informed by biases, and the tricky thing is that we're often unaware of them. Our brains are wired to conserve resources, so they take shortcuts, rapidly putting people and things into categories, and assigning attributes to those categories informed by societal, sociological, and historical constructs of race, gender, sexual orientation, or class. Certain groups are labeled as easy-going, others as smart, still others as threatening.

In particular, we have to watch out for affinity bias, the unconscious tendency to get along with people who are like us. In other words, we gravitate toward people with similar appearances, beliefs, and backgrounds. When colleagues aren't like us—perhaps in terms of gender, race, ethnicity, education, physical abilities, position at work—we are more likely to feel ambivalent about them. That's why it's critical when we're struggling with a coworker to ask ourselves: "What role could bias be playing here? Is it possible I'm not seeing the situation clearly because we're different in certain ways?"

Play devil's advocate with yourself, repeatedly asking whether you're seeing your colleague's behavior impartially. Use the *flip it to test it* approach: If your colleague was a different gender, race, sexual orientation, would you make the same assumptions? Or be willing to say the same things or treat them the same way? This technique was introduced to me by Kristen Pressner, a global HR executive, who confessed to having certain prejudices about women leaders in her TEDx talk.[9] To interrupt her own bias, especially when she finds herself judging a woman in power, she substitutes a man into the situation and sees if she holds the same view.

Watch for Mixed Messages

Chances are that if you feel ambivalent about your colleague, you're probably behaving inconsistently toward them too. It takes two to tango. Perhaps, for example, because you've inadvertently signaled to your coworker that you don't like direct confrontation, they occasionally resort to passive-aggressive tactics to get their point across. Keep in mind that your reactions may be equally destabilizing to them.

It's tempting to go down the spiral of who is causing more of the problem. But it doesn't matter who created the tension in the first place; it matters who is going to make the choice to change it.

Focus on Your Goal

It's important to be clear with yourself about what you want from your relationship with your frenemy. Identifying your goal will help you stay focused on constructive tactics. Do you want to complete the project you've been working on together and move on? Have a healthy working relationship that will last into the future? Feel less angry or frustrated after interacting with them? Or do you want to let their behavior get under your skin less often? Or do you want them to stop undermining your success?

I recommend making a list of the goals you'd like to achieve (big and small) and then circling the one, two, or three that are most important. Your intentions will determine—subconsciously and consciously— how you act. Just make sure your goal is realistic. Transforming a frenemy into a friend isn't always possible. But you can try to make sure you're aligned more often, and you consistently demonstrate respect for one another.

In the same vein, consider whether you can align yourself with your colleague, so you're focused on the same goal. Joining forces could help channel your collective talents and energy in positive ways. And since frenemies can be a source of motivation, you may find yourself spurred to work harder on the given task. Is there a project you can tackle together? Or a problem you can help them solve? Of course, teaming up may be unappealing. Who would want to put themselves directly in the line of fire? But spending time together may help ease the tension and allow you to develop more empathy for one another.

Emphasize the Positive

It's possible to decrease the ambivalence in your relationship by focusing on the positive interactions that you do have. And making that aspect of your relationship apparent to the other person. For example, you might mention ways that you've supported them behind-the-scenes (recommended them for a high-profile project, for example, or backed up their idea about how to make up this quarter's budget shortfall). You might also call out positive interactions you do have, expressing, for example, how happy you were that you all collaborated on a recent initiative that increased revenue for your division. Highlighting the good side of your relationship may help your colleague see your overall dynamic in a more positive light and decrease the level of ambivalence you both feel, putting your relationship on more stable ground going forward.

Occupying Frenemy Territory

None of our relationships are fixed. We might assume that the positive ones will always stay that way and the ambivalent or negative ones are doomed to be torturous forever. But that mindset can lead us to neglect our work friendships, and completely dismiss the more complicated ones. Fortunately, ambivalent relationships, especially in times of uncertainty, don't need to be sources of ongoing strife. By following the tactics I've laid out above, you can both change the way you see and feel about the relationship—and take concrete steps to improve it.

Biography

Amy Gallo is a contributing editor at *Harvard Business Review* and author of *Getting Along: How to Work with Anyone (Even Difficult People)* and the *HBR Guide to Dealing with Conflict*. In 2023, she was named to the Thinkers50 Radar list of up-and-coming thinkers whose ideas could make a positive difference in the world.

Notes

1. Andrew Parker, Alexandra Gerbasi, and Christine L. Porath, "The Effects of De-Energizing Ties in Organizations and How to Manage Them," *Organizational Dynamics*, 42(2) (April–June 2013): 110–118. https://doi.org/10.1016/j.orgdyn.2013.03.004.
2. Jessica R. Methot, Shimul Melwani, and Naomi B. Rothman, "The Space Between Us: A Social-Functional Emotions View of Ambivalent and

Indifferent Workplace Relationships," *Journal of Management*, 43(6) (January 2017): 1789–1819. https://doi.org/10.1177/0149206316685853.

3. Bert N. Uchino, Julianne Holt-Lunstad, Darcy Uno, et al., "Heterogeneity in the Social Networks of Young and Older Adults: Prediction of Mental Health and Cardiovascular Reactivity During Acute Stress," *Journal of Behavioral Medicine*, 24 (2001): 361–382. https://link.springer.com/article/10.1023/A:1010634902498.

4. Julianne Holt-Lunstad, Bert N. Uchino, Timothy W. Light, et al., "On the Importance of Relationship Quality: The Impact of Ambivalence in Friendships on Cardiovascular Functioning," *Annals of Behavioral Medicine*, 33(3) (2007): 361–382. http://europepmc.org/article/MED/17600455; Bert N. Uchino, Richard Cawthon, Timothy W. Light, et al., "Social Relationships and Health: Is Feeling Positive, Negative, or Both (Ambivalent) About Your Social Ties Related to Telomeres?" *Health Psychology*, 31(6) (2012): 789–796. https://psycnet.apa.org/buy/2012-00041-001.

5. Shimul Melwani and Naomi B. Rothman, "The Push-and-Pull of Frenemies: When and Why Ambivalent Relationships Lead to Helping and Harming," *Journal of Applied Psychology*, 107(5) (May 2022): 707–723. https://pubmed.ncbi.nlm.nih.gov/34570565/.

6. Ibid.

7. F. Scott Fitzgerald, "The Crack-Up," https://www.google.com/books/edition/The_Crack_up/B8saLwl-2TEC?hl=en&gbpv=1&bsq=intelligence.

8. Adam Grant, "Opinion: The Science of Changing Someone's Mind," *New York Times*, https://www.nytimes.com/2021/01/31/opinion/change-someones-mind.html.

9. Kristen Pressner, "Are You Biased? I Am," filmed May 2016 at TEDxBasel, Basel, Basel-Stadt, Switzerland, video. https://www.youtube.com/watch?v=Bq_xYSOZrgU&vl=en.

27

How Leaders Can Help
Employees Face Uncertainty

Ben Whitter

The world has been rocked by multifaceted challenges that have converged to disrupt economies and the health, and well-being of citizens. No one has escaped. It has been a shared experience the world over. With costs for basic living necessities spiraling, the aftershocks of a global pandemic still being suffered alongside war in Europe, a major recession being predicted and increasing political division, employees have faced extreme levels of uncertainty. Firms have changed and so too have their workplaces with increasingly flexible and disruptive work models.

Uncertainty is an interesting mix of speculation and possibility. A lot of information is under review and that thinking starts to show up in actions and behaviors of companies, people, and institutions. This trickles down to daily lives—uncertainty with gas and energy supplies drives up prices at forecourts and supermarkets. Uncertainty about how global events will impact firms reshapes decisions and investments. This vicious back and forth between supply and demand naturally hits consumer confidence, which in turn, hits profitability and productivity. If people are uncertain, they stop buying and start saving. This then makes companies uncertain; they stop innovating and investing, which affects growth, performance, and ultimately, jobs and livelihoods. The dance goes on—everything is connected.

Uncertain Times, Uncertain Leadership

It doesn't always feel like everything links up in a nice and neat manner. Indeed, uncertainty, in large part, is driven by systems and people that are dependent on each other yet remain disconnected in the minds of leaders and decision-makers. It's the same within companies; leaders don't often see as their problem to solve the human experience and all the challenges their people face. Traditionally, there has been no role for the manager outside of the 9–5 work schedule. It just simply wasn't any of their business what difficulties people were facing, and nor did they want it to be. While self-reliance is an almighty practice for people to live in their hearts, minds, and deeds, the nature and scale of the challenges being experienced by people are often a deciding factor in how productive they will be at work. Overwhelming personal issues and uncertainty are not the best foundations for employee success. Couple this with a lack of general understanding, empathy and support from leadership and things get worse, not better.

Yet, managers don't have magic wands and it is unlikely that they can resolve complex global challenges affecting their employees. So, what can they do to guide people *through* uncertain times? In my research, I found that the most effective way to support employees is to zoom in on all the roles that they play in life, and, with empathy and compassion, provide the best possible help in the moments that matter to them. This is a highly personalized way of leading and enables managers to meet people where they are in life. Indeed, at uncertain times, we need to see much more humanity from people in leadership roles.

What roles are we talking about? The Human Role model, which is based on extensive global research for my book, *Human Experience at Work*,[1] documents the roles that people are most concerned with as part of their human experience. And to build on that, we can see some clear manager actions that are vital when dealing with uncertainty (Table 27.1).

Table 27.1 Managers' role in dealing with uncertainty

Role	Manager actions
EXPLORER	Leaders give people time and space to explore and adapt to changing circumstances providing guidance, direction, and a supportive high-trust work environment. They encourage self-exploration and respond to the new expectations that people have about work. They also respect organizational boundaries and give people opportunities and a safe place to experiment with new ideas or new approaches to business.
CONTRIBUTOR	Leaders coach, guide, and facilitate in real time to help people deliver their strongest contribution to the company and the community around them. Leaders are proactive when it comes to removing organizational barriers that stand in the way of people making a positive contribution.
CITIZEN	Leaders are sensitive and aware of challenges in society and the wider economy, and how these impact employees. They use this awareness to deliver personalized support at the right time. They meet the moment and connect people (and their work) to positive outcomes for the planet and their community.
CARER	Leaders tailor their management approach to the individual and their unique circumstances taking into account the employee's other responsibilities. Every employee cares for someone or something in life—leaders help them to carry out this role through a flexible, supportive, and responsive employee experience.
PERFORMER	Leaders co-create with employees to enable strong performance. It's not about objectives by diktat. The management relationship is founded on collaboration and a co-created team experience. Performance is enhanced through practices that demonstrate transparency and trust.
ARCHITECT	Leaders give people autonomy and greater control over their work, their roles, and their lives. Leadership is about delivering outcomes and employees have the backing to become masters of their craft and their own employee experience.

(Source: Ben Whitter ©, *Human Role Model*.)

The Business Case for Human-Centered Leadership

Despite uncertainty in society or the economy, we can be absolutely certain that human-centered leaders deliver more performance, more productivity, more profitability, and more innovation from their teams than any other type of leader. We know this, don't we? From our own experiences we can easily identify the leaders who successfully enabled our best performances. Unfortunately, it is also extremely easy to spot the leaders who hindered our progress and performance outcomes as human beings, and negatively affected us in some way.

Uncertainty can be advantageous and used impactfully by managers to fuel success, personal growth, and achievement. Leaders can leverage it to build high-performing and enjoyable team environments where people are not afraid to be human. They can try things, they can fail forward into success, and they can cement a sense of togetherness and a sense of belonging that becomes a defining career memory. Indeed, employment relationships borne out of crisis, adversity, and uncertainty become catalysts for resilient and high-performing teams and people over the long term.

Alongside this personalized and human-centered leadership style, there is the chance to do other things that make a fundamental difference to people at times of uncertainty. Frankly, it is to lead in a way that it is hopeful, optimistic, positive, moral, and to consistently relieve the unease and anxiety across the workforce by being someone whom they can believe in. No hype. No gimmicks. No PR. Just a decent person who cares about people and does the right thing by them. Do we really need a business case to justify doing the right thing?

Clearly, the Patagonia founder Yvon Chouinard doesn't think so, given he has just given away his entire company to the planet. "As of now, Earth is our only shareholder," the company announced. "ALL profits, in perpetuity, will go to our mission to 'save our home planet'."[2]

Positive activism starts with words, but the work really begins with actions. This big, bold action demonstrates the power that leadership can have and the good that it can do. Now, from a CEO/founder position it can be easier, but it's simply a matter of scale. This CEO asked himself what he could do, what he could design, and what role his organization could play in the most uncertain of times for the planet, and he came up with an ambitious co-created plan that inspired hope, advocacy, and admiration all over the world. As a manager this can be done—it's just the scale that changes. Leaders can make their contribution by creating more certainty within their teams and companies through what they permit, what they promote, and what they support.

Leading through uncertainty is taking decisions and making moves that elevate the human spirit and the connection that people have with each other, their organizations, and the world they live in. This, for me, is real business progress. When we think less about me, and more about we, and we demonstrate our leadership through exceptional actions.

Turning Points: Moments That Matter

Given the economic uncertainty in the global economy, employees worldwide are looking to their leaders and organizations for support that goes beyond business as usual. Leadership that reaches into the depths of the human experience and support provided at crisis moments means more to people. Indeed, one in twenty big businesses understand this and have been scrambling to provide cost-of-living bonuses—and in some cases, pay rises—to staff to help with soaring energy costs over winter.[3] They could have done nothing. They chose to do something to bring about an uplift in certainty across their workforces.

This flows into the next point about leading through uncertainty; it is best managed, whether at individual, managerial or organization levels, by doing something useful that actually helps people when they need it most. That is the defining feeling when I speak to employees about this. They respect timely, positive, and concrete support. Words may well be comforting, but actions resonate the most.

Offering words of encouragement, resilience training or yoga workshops don't cut it. When leaders identify pain points that are affecting people and their performance, something has to be done, and fast. Leaders need to meet the moment head-on and not be found wanting. At every stage, employees will be looking for definitive symbols and signs across their organization that points to a leadership team that cares and they can trust. Without the actions alongside this, no amount of fancy rhetoric will make the path though uncertainty any easier.

Leaders We Can Trust

If employees believe in a brighter future, it's because senior leaders have helped enable that feeling. But in the bigger scheme of things, trust in immediate management is the far more powerful indicator (and predictor) of future engagement and performance. As I've found in my extensive research in the employee experience field, companies can have the best facilities, the best IT, the best infrastructure, the best CEO, the best technology, and the best of everything else, but if the employee's relationship with their direct supervisor isn't solid, then all of that won't make the difference it was meant to. Trust in our immediate managers is of utmost importance in the employee experience, especially during times of uncertainty.

The final recommendation then for anyone fortunate enough and privileged to be in a leadership position is to be someone people can *trust*. I'm talking rock solid trust with values and morals to match. Employees don't need any more uncertainty on top of what they're dealing with right now so one of the biggest differentiators of high-performing leaders is simply the fact that people believe what they say because their actions, habits, and behaviors match up. For that reason, the development of a healthy character, disposition, or as Aristotle put it, *hexis*, should continue to be a primetime area to explore within leadership development.

In a chaotic and unbelievable world, leaders who role-model the purpose, mission, and values of their brands—and get the fundamental basics of being a good person right—will create a very welcome aura and atmosphere of stability.

Biography

Ben Whitter is the CEO of HEX Organization, which supports leading brands and employers in developing their holistic, human-centered and experience-driven capabilities. The author of *Employee Experience*, he is the creator of the Holistic Employee Experience (HEX) model. In 2021, he was named to the Thinkers50 Radar list of 30 up-and-coming thinkers whose ideas could make a positive difference in the world.

Notes

1. Ben Whitter, *Human Experience at Work* (London: Kogan Page, 2021).
2. https://www.patagonia.com/ownership/.
3. https://news.sky.com/story/one-in-20-big-businesses-have-offered-workers-a-cost-of-living-bonus-12670385.

About the Editor

Des Dearlove is an internationally recognized expert on management thinking. Together with Stuart Crainer, he founded Thinkers50, which for more than two decades has championed the very best management ideas.

A former columnist for *The Times* (London) and contributing editor to *Strategy+Business*, Des is the co-editor of the *Financial Times Handbook of Management* and the co-author of several best-selling books, including *Gravy Training: Inside the Business of Business Schools*, and *Generation Entrepreneur*, which was shortlisted for the WH Smith's Business Book of the Year Award. His books have been translated into more than 20 languages.

Des has taught at some of the world's leading business schools, including IE Business School and the Said Business School at Oxford University, where he is an Associate Fellow. Under the pen name of D. D. Everest, he is also the author of the *Archie Greene* trilogy of children's books, which was shortlisted for the National Book Awards Children's Book of the Year.

Acknowledgments

I'd like to thank all of those who contributed to this book in one form or another.

I'm especially indebted to the members of the Thinkers50 community who shared their insights: Sheree Atcheson, Ori Brafman, Rom Brafman, Paul R. Carlile, Julie Carrier, Kirstin Ferguson, Nathan Furr, Susannah Harmon Furr, Amy Gallo, Matt Gitsham, Ruth Gotian, Mehran Gul, Diane Hamilton, Maja Korica, Marianne W. Lewis, David Liddle, Terence Mauri, Jennifer Moss, Gorick Ng, David Nour, Leon C. Prieto, Simone T.A. Phipps, Benjamin Pring, Megan Reitz, Wendy K. Smith, Lisa Kay Solomon, Modupe Taylor-Pearce, Tamsen Webster, Ben Whitter, Andrew Winston, and Kai D. Wright.

I'd also like to thank Amy Edmondson for writing the Foreword, and for her continuing support of the Thinkers50 mission, and Shannon Vargo and her team at Wiley, Jeanenne Ray, Jozette Moses, and Michelle Hacker, for their enthusiasm for this project and for being such great partners.

My thanks also to the amazing team at Thinkers50: Lisa Humphries, who helped edit the contributions, Monika Kosman, Adina Rizga, and Mercy Tapscott. And, of course, to Stuart Crainer, for sharing the Thinkers50 journey with me.

Index

Page numbers followed by *f* and *t* refer to figures and tables, respectively.